At the End
of the Day

A Memoir

EVERETT WOOLUM

At the End of the Day

A Memoir of

Everett Woolum

WORKBOOK PRESS LLC
187 E Warm Springs Rd,
Suite B285 Las Vegas NV 89119 USA

Website: https://workbookpress.com/
Hotline: 1-888-818-4856
Email: admin@workbookpress.com

Ordering Information:

Quantity sales. Special discounts are available on quantity purchases by corporations, associations, and others. For details, contact the publisher at the address above.

Library of Congress Control Number:

ISBN-13:   978-1-965732-29-8   Paperback Version
                978-1-965732-30-4   Digital Version

REV. DATE: 03/19/2025

DEDICATION

For my family and friends.

Contents

Preface

Writing a memoir is a major task which one does not undertake lightly. My relatives kept asking me to write my memoirs because they were interested in my life. My close friend, Gustavo Serra, has also encouraged me to leave an account for my family and others.

So much history and experience is lost as older generations pass away. With the demise of the "nuclear family" and as relatives move away, the ability to recount family lore and heritage through storytelling has been lost. This memoir is an attempt to pass down my story in written form.

I have written about what I know of my parents' lives. In spite of the hardships they endured, they played a strong role in influencing my early childhood and that of my siblings. Since my parents passed years ago, I have little access to early family records. Nonetheless, I have attempted to collect information from as many sources as possible. This memoir, which you now hold, is the culmination of my efforts.

Why do so many people write life stories to explain themselves and their experiences? I believe that they want to share their deepest thoughts, feelings and experiences. In other words, they want to leave a legacy.

At 96, I'm telling it like it is. "At the end of the day", I'm reflecting back on my childhood and my careers in the military, aerospace and real estate. I also discuss my marriage and family life as well as my travel experiences. Along the way, I hope to impart principles of success and effective leadership and other important life-lessons.

Lastly, many of my relatives and friends might want to know about our common DNA. If you are interested, I have a separate booklet that describes my 23andMe profile.

I hope you'll benefit from reading my life's story. This is my legacy that I leave for you.

Everett Woolum

Acknowledgments

A special thank-you is in order to my wife, Mary Ann, for being an excellent partner, one that I could always depend upon in any situation, a solid rock in support of our life together.

I greatly appreciate the contribution that Brenda, my daughter, for her role in converting my handwritten noted into a useable Word format that assisted in the production of this memoir.

It is with great pleasure that I acknowledge the significant contribution made by Gustavo Serra, for his work in editing and for his never-ending encouragement in my effort to complete this project.

I am deeply grateful To Dr. Rosita K. Serra for our close friendship through the years while managing rentals, traveling, taking college classes, dancing lessons, going to parties and participating in local activities.

I am indebted to Miss Willow Hopkins for her friendship and for being my excellent realtor for 42 years.

I want to thank my mother, father, brothers, sisters and relatives for their help during times of hardships and celebrations. I would not be who I am without you.

A very special thank-you is in order to my editor, Denis Ledoux and the Production Manager, Sally Lunt of The Memoir Network (info@ thememoirnetwork.com). They are professionals with a keen, critical eye for language usage, grammar, story-telling and overall vision for the project.

Everett Woolum

CHAPTER 1

My Family Origin

My family came to the United States to escape religious strife in Germany. In the eighteenth century, Catholics and Protestants struggled against each other and rampant conflicts led to much blood shedding. Ulm, Germany, the town where my ancestors originated, was not any different. My first ancestor to come to America, Martin Ulm, was an orphan who had been committed to an orphanage. It is believed that his parents were deceased and that he and his two sisters had become wards of a religious group. The religious conflicts continued to be dangerous enough that, around 1751, it was agreed by the leaders of their religious faith to transfer children, among whom were Martin Ulm, my then-five-year-old great-great-great-grandfather, and his sisters, out of this stricken area and send them to America. For this journey, the children were accompanied by an adult religious escort.

When the three young immigrants went through customs in Baltimore, Maryland, their last name was changed from Ulm to many misinterpretations, such as Woodlum, Wollum, Wolum and similar spellings. Their name was finally settled as Woolum, which is used today.

The children and their escort settled in Loudoun, Virginia, an area not far from Baltimore. Martin and his sisters, according to family lore, adjusted to the new environment very well.

In the British colonies, the Ulm children grew into adulthood and worked diligently while coping with the many challenges of a new environment. Martin married, (Elizabeth – last name unknown) and had a child named Andrew, who was born in Loudoun, Virginia, in 1768. Andrew married in Virginia but eventually moved westward with his family. He traveled through West Virginia, Virginia, Tennessee and eventually into Kentucky which he reached through the Cumberland Gap route around 1795.

Arriving in Knox County, Kentucky, Andrew found the land to be fertile and ideal for farming so he decided to settle there and make a home. The State name is believed to come from the Native American word *geda'geh (meaning, "meadow")* which the settlers pronounced Kentucky. By the time the white settlers arrived down the Ohio River and through the Cumberland Gap (10 to 12 miles from where I grew up) there weren't many Native Americans left.

Andrew had 8 children: John, James, Elizabeth, Rebecca, Jacob, Samuel, Mary and Sallie. Samuel, my great-great-grandfather, was born in 1800 in Virginia and died in Jenson, Kentucky in 1890. Samuel had 10 children, Elizabeth, John, Sarah, Calbina, Nancy, Mary, Frances, China (my grandmother), Emily and Charity; all were born in Harlan County, Kentucky, near my hometown of Jenson. The descendants of Andrew's children spread over the area. Because of the poor communication facilities at the time I was growing up, I did not know this extended family.

Jenson, the community where I was born, consisted of scattered family cabins in southeastern Kentucky. This is Appalachian Mountain country where most land was hard to work but the bottom land was found to be productive and good for farming. There were large wooded areas which allowed for plentiful hunting and collecting of wood for heating, cooking and construction. The lower valley, carved out by a small river, provided clean water and some fish to supplement the food produced by farming and hunting. Corn, hemp and tobacco were the main crops grown by the first settlers in Kentucky who exhibited a pioneering spirit that characterized parts of Kentucky into my childhood. Horse racing, breeding and riding were also part of the cultural fabric of Kentucky. Kentuckians loved horses which they used for transportation, labor and racing.

China, my grandmother, who was one of Samuel's daughters, was born in 1842 and died in 1923 in Jenson, Kentucky. Her one child, Skelton Woolum, born in 1862, was my father. He was born and was raised by China, a 20-year-old single mother. China never married. As was the usual custom for children born out of wedlock at the time, my father took the name of Woolum from his mother. My father's birth was a "hushed up affair" because having children out of wedlock back then was a no-no and no one would talk about the situation. My Father's father, Ansa Ward, lived in Four Mile, Kentucky, two miles from Jenson, Kentucky. Ansa was never part of my father's life.

My father had nine children by his first wife, Lydia Woolum. Their children were Laura, Robert, Sadie, Mary, Charley, William, Leonard, Rosa and Lucy. They are all deceased.

After Lydia passed away, my father was at some loss as to how to raise 9 children alone. My mother, Maudie Ellen Slusher, for her part, wanted to leave Red Bird, a town about seventeen miles away. She seems to have been out of sorts with her family, and wanting to get away, she heard of a man who was looking for a housekeeper. He could not have been offering much by way of financial compensation, but my mother was not seeking much either. They probably agreed on room and board and some small salary. Eventually as a result of living under the same roof, and in spite of the thirty-year age difference, they grew to respect each other and to realize they could marry which is just what they did. Eventually they had four children together: Virgil, Pauline, Everett and Christine.

At 5'7", my father was not a big man but he made up for his small stature with a strong work ethic and steely determination. Nothing came easy to him. His mustached face showed the strain of a hard life. Although he always wore a hat for protection, his sun and wind-weathered skin hinted at long hours of outdoor work. From the morning's first light until nightfall he would toil to provide for his growing family.

My father, who had a third-grade education and could only write his name and read a few simple sentences knew no other life than farming.

Skelton Woolum, father, circa 1927

Education seemed to be a luxury that he and local folks could not imagine they could ever have use for. The struggle for survival was his primary concern. Don't ever confuse a lack of formal education with a lack of intelligence, however. Folks in those days had to be able to improvise and devise tools to fix the many problems and issues they faced. This meant that they had to be self-reliant and plenty smart to survive their austere circumstances and eke out a living from the land.

The comforts we now take for granted did not exist. When I was growing up, there was no electricity for lights, gas for cooking and heating, or indoor plumbing; the work to bring in needed supplies was never-ending and the days were mostly taken up in growing and gathering provisions for basic survival.

The household was ably managed by my mother, Maudie Ellen Slusher Woolum. Born in 1892 and so 30 years my father's junior, she provided for the family by working a small garden through the spring and summer and canning vegetables for the long winter months. Maudie had a 5th grade education. She could read and write a little, as well as sign her name. She was a Christian woman who attended church and Sunday School regularly. She had an excellent disposition and was an outstanding wife and mother.

I think that my parents had a good to excellent marriage. I can't say if they had a loving relationship but I can say that they respected each other. I didn't hear or see any type of disrespectful exchanges, no arguments or bad mouthing from either as they got along very well.

Both my mother and father were strict disciplinarians and would not hesitate to use a switch, belt, or other means to instill discipline in us children. They were both hard-working, honest folks who taught their children the value of work, education and good character.

Skelton and Maudie, circa 1942

Family feuds were common in the Appalachian Mountains. The mountainous region of southeastern Kentucky was one of the earliest "frontier-towns" in the United States. This region lacked well-established law and order. Courts and law enforcement officials existed, but the topography of the region and the sparsely distributed population made enforcing the law difficult. The people distrusted the courts.

Bitter disputes arose over a variety of matters such as, livestock, women, politics and thievery. The straying of livestock, the wronging of a woman or the killing of a dog could set friend against friend, family against family and neighbors against neighbors.

During the Civil War, Kentucky was a border state between the North and South, and it remained within the Union. Jenson was not too far from Virginia and Tennessee, both of which were Confederate States. This too, was a source of heated arguments. When he was around 4 years old, my father saw a Union soldier, in uniform, scouting and patrolling the area near his home.

As I grew up, folks would still argue over the Civil War. Since Kentucky was one of the dividing states between the North and South, even close neighbors might have backed one side, or the other... Another reason to quarrel.

Occasionally, I had the opportunity to go to the nearby town of Pineville on Saturdays to watch a Hopalong Cassidy or a Lone Ranger film. These western movies were offered for five cents. While walking along the streets, bullets would sometimes ring over our heads. A drunk hillbilly who was apparently feuding with a neighbor had decided to open fire. People would take cover inside the nearest building. Since the region was so unruly, we would often ask "Who got killed today?" The most famous of the mountain feuds was the Hatfield-McCoy (1880-1887). As a result of this volatile feuding, my father always had a weapon nearby for protection.

During Prohibition, most families made "home brew", a form of strong whiskey, and fought back against the government prohibition established by the 18th Amendment to the US Constitution. Even though my family never made whiskey, or drank it, my parents and us children had to be careful because the daily disruptions caused by this unrest swirled all around us and the community. Our family stayed away from making trouble. As a result, the Woolums are characterized by being calm, law-abiding, productive members of society.

CHAPTER 2

My Childhood

Early in the morning of February 27, 1929, I was born to Skelton and Maudie Woolum in a two-room log cabin in Jenson, Kentucky, a town in southeastern Kentucky. I was delivered by mid-wife and neighbor Alice Hendrickson who saw that, my "eyes shown and sparkled like a diamond" and so suggested to the doctor that I be named *Diamond Everett Woolum*. My parents didn't object and thought that this was an appropriate name. Apparently, the doctor did not agree as he did not write my name as planned on the birth certificate but only entered *Everett Woolum*. My parents did not discover this error until after the information was recorded. As a result, I did not acquire a middle name. My mother and Mrs. Hendrickson said I was very active and alert and progressed very rapidly after birth.

When my mother was weaning me from nursing, she decided to visit her sister for a few days without me. I was already big for a child that needed weaning but I did not like solid food. What was my mother to do? She decided that, if she were not there, I would get hungry enough and start eating solids. She left me, and after a few days, returned home. When I saw her, I ran after her crying, "I'm hungry, I'm hungry," but she held firm and eventually I was weaned.

The part of Kentucky where we lived was largely unsettled, mountainous terrain with some valley land for farming, but the area was overgrown and difficult to farm. Several sides of mountain were cleared to allow for certain crops to be planted such as corn and other vegetables for a family garden. All members of my family put their shoulder to the wheel and worked hard to raise food to feed everyone.

The six of us—my parents and four siblings—resided in the two-room log cabin my father had built. Flooring had been installed two or three years before I was born, but before that people lived right on the dirt of the ground—which gives meaning to the term "ground floor!" We did not have running water or indoor toilets much less

Typical Kentucky Log Cabin, similar to our home.

central heating, inside showers or air-conditioning. Eventually, my parents added a kitchen to the structure and thus created a third room.

Our mattresses were made with chicken feathers so we called them feather beds. These mattresses were soft and kept our body warm during the winter but they also were a perfect breeding ground for bed bugs. During the summer months, my mother would move the mattresses outside in the direct sunlight to kill the bugs or at least drive them away.

My mother, who was very religious, took us to church and Sunday School whenever the roving Baptist minister came to Jenson. We did not have a church building, but the minister would conduct services and Sunday School in a nearby county school building. Across Straight Creek, the small stream in front of our house, there was a Pentecostal church. During certain periods and occasions, the members of this congregation would handle snakes, jump over the benches and chairs and sometimes run outside—all the while proclaiming that they were worshiping the Lord. A lot of people would come to the Pentecostal services to observe these unusual activities. We did not attend this church because it was not our faith; we were Baptists.

When I was around 4 years old, I was climbing through a window that was propped up with a stick. I accidentally dislodged the stick and the window fell on the little finger on my left hand, nearly cut the tip off. My sister, Pauline, comforted me for days and weeks while I recuperated. I did not see a doctor about this accident because we could not afford one. In my first 17 years, I only saw a doctor once when I broke an arm at the age of 10, while playing leapfrog. Our fallback was always to use home remedies.

Although the kindergarten was only about 400 or 500 yards from our house, my mother walked with me to school. After the session, she came and walked me back home. This was the procedure until I got accustomed to the teachers, the other children and the new surroundings. As I began to demonstrate an ability to get to school on time and to come back home safely, she stopped accompanying me.

Everett, circa 1935

As I grew in size and age, I was given more responsibility: building fires in the winter, feeding the livestock, milking the cows and working in the garden. When I was 5 years old, going barefoot as most kids did during summer, was an enjoyable experience... But it also allowed my shoes to last, since I only got new shoes about every three years. At 5, I was also a water boy, carrying drinking water to my parents and two older siblings who were tending the crops in the field. At around 7 or 8 years old, I was given a job at school to build fires each morning in the two potbelly stoves. I was paid five cents for each fire. I collected kindling wood during the summer with the anticipation that I would again get the job in the fall, when school resumed. The start of a new school year meant that I would, once again get to play marbles with the boys and play tag with both boys and girls. We did not have running water in the school so the teacher would ask the children to carry water from a well for the us to drink while in class. The class work, the games and the chores, all contributed to a great feeling of teamwork and self-reliance for me—It made me feel appreciated and satisfied. I was very proud of the responsibility I had, and the money I earned for building those school fires. I saved those pennies for years. Some would say that I still have those first few cents I earned.

In my childhood, each day was pretty much just like another day. Even the holidays, during which we still had to feed the animals and to bring wood in to heat the cabin. We did not get a break from the routine. At Christmas, we would hang our stockings on the fireplace mantle for Santa Claus to fill. The presents were much the same from year to year, an orange, an apple, a banana and some nuts. This was all we expected, and we were very happy to get these items.

When I was 7 or 8 years old, I decided to see if I could catch Santa as he climbed down the chimney to fill our stocking hanging from the mantle. I sat up all night but Santa never came. Because of my spying, I did not receive any Christmas presents in my stocking that year... A hard lesson to learn! Around this time, I also began to collect the cows and lead them back to the barn to feed and milk. I fed chickens and hogs, too. Work on our farm was almost always demanding. We did not have many conveniences, even by standards of the day. Take laundry for instance, on Wednesdays, my mother would build fires in the outside pit to boil water to wash our clothes. The hot water was placed in the tub, and using a washboard my mother would devote much of the day to laundering our family's clothes. She would periodically throw the soiled water away, and after heating more water would begin a new batch. On these days, if I was home, I might be called upon to get more firewood to heat water. There was always something to do. As the clothing was washed, she would hang it on a long outdoor clothesline for the sun and the wind to dry. When a rainstorm fell on the farm, the laundry might have to stay outside for another day.

By the fifth grade, I helped with bailing hay. In the seventh grade, I was strong enough to handle horses for plowing. By then, I was responsible for all types of farm chores with my father as Virgil was often away either at college or teaching. The same was true of Pauline. My father was in his late 70s, and I am certain he appreciated the work I could do. Permitting the two older children to pursue their school goals was another way my family demonstrated their support of education. I'm sure their being away so much posed a hardship on my father and mother.

The school system I knew in Kentucky in those early years and into the 1940s was structured in three levels: primary, secondary and post-secondary education. In primary and secondary schools, students started at 5 to 6 years of age and generally ended their educations anywhere from 16 to 18, depending on the school system, state policy and student progress. There may have been a pre-school unit but this was not required as was primary and secondary schooling. All children were guaranteed the right to a free public elementary and secondary education when living within jurisdiction of the United States regardless of race, gender, ability, status, religion or economic condition, but of course, not all children were able to avail themselves of this opportunity. Many withdrew at some point before finishing to earn income to help their families.

As already mentioned, the two-room country public school building was within walking distance from our home. One room was devoted to grades 1 through 4 while the other room housed grades 5 through 8. In each room, there was a teacher who was responsible for teaching all subjects. This arrangement, with multiple grades and subjects being taught in one room, did not allow for a good teaching, or learning situation. There was no library and only a few text books provided by the county. In addition, the children were sometimes unruly. In primary school, children were disciplined by spanking with a paddle, by expulsion or by having to write a sentence 100 times.

During recess and breaks, students were encouraged to participate in sports, and I did so. Most of the time, sports and games were not organized by the teacher. It was all very informal: we chose sides during recess and lunch to make pick-up teams to play touch football in the late summer and fall and softball in the early spring and summer. Sometimes, we boys would play tackle football, but the teachers did not like for us to do so because of possible injury. On one occasion, in fact, when playing tackle football, I lunged my head in the concrete foundation of the school building. The only damage, fortunately, was a skinned-up face and head. As the short stop in softball, I could scoop up the fast-travelling ball, throw it to first base before the batter arrived and get an immediate out. Virgil told me, if I continued this performance, I would someday be in the majors. Of course, I liked to hear that.

Back then, it was especially hard for some children to get through primary school, because of the Depression. There was tremendous pressure on children to quit school and help on the farm. Because of this, not everyone progressed to high school even though there were no entrance exams required to advance. My family felt the same economic pressures, except that my parents wanted us to continue in school. My father had a third-grade education, my mother a fifth, but they realized the importance of educating their children and encouraged each of us to maximize our potential and abilities. We had little money for paper, pencils or books, but my parents managed somehow to provide us with what we needed and to keep us focused on our education.

While in the two-room grade school, I had a friend I thought of as a girlfriend. Her name was Erma Lee Swartz. She lived within our community, but I only saw her when we were in school. After grade school, her parents moved Erma Lee to a high school in Pineville, a city school. Although Pineville is only about four and half miles from Jenson, we lost contact. I found out later that she married a man about 20 years older and died quite young—only a few years after marrying.

My father and brother-in-law, Cam Elliott, owned a farm 30 miles away in Barboursville, Knox County, Kentucky. One day when I was with them in a cornfield, during a brief period when we were resting the animals after a rapid plowing, a man came on the scene and said that he lived nearby. He was a professor at Union College which was not far away from our field. We started chatting, and after a few minutes, he told us his take about the Sears catalogue ordering procedure. To place an order from a Sears catalogue, a person had to be able to read the instructions, enter the information on the order form, calculate the total cost, address and mail the envelope. This man felt, if a person could place an order and receive the right merchandise, that this person was an educated man. Not many older people in that day and age in Kentucky could order a product using a Sears catalogue. While this man's statement has stuck with me for over 80 years, that day was the first and only time I saw this gentleman. As far as my own goals were concerned, I certainly wanted my education to add up to more than being able to order from a Sears catalog!

Union College was a small liberal arts college which my brother Virgil, 12 years older than I, and my sister Pauline, 9 years older than I, had attended. (Prior to college, Virgil had graduated from high school as valedictorian of his class and Pauline as salutatorian of hers.) Union had a program which provided teaching credentials after one year of college. Virgil earned this minimum credential and started teaching at grade school in Kentucky. He would teach one year to earn money to attend college the next year,

This rotation continued for Virgil for a few years in the late 1930s, while I was still a boy. When he started teaching, he was 18 or 19 years old. As a result, parents who had very little education thought that they could tell him how to teach and push him around. They did not appreciate young Virgil correcting their children. These parents threatened him several times and tried to force him to quit, but he stood his ground and continued teaching. The parents eventually backed off. After that year he resumed college and after a few more years of experience, at other locations, he was appointed assistant high school principal at a small rural community in Kentucky. In that way, Virgil received his bachelor's degree in education while gaining experience. His commitment to education made an impression on me.

One of the tangible ways that my father and mother demonstrated their support for education was helping Virgil and Pauline to buy a new Ford car to use for transportation to and from Union College. Each paid $200.00 for their part of the total cost. This was a lot of money then, but the Ford provided them needed transportation. They drove the car, which sometimes did not even have enough power to go up steep hills. While living at home, going to school one year and teaching school the next year, they alternated this process until they finished college; all the time, I was watching their activities and letting their example model my own future.

While my brother and sister were breaking new ground in the family by going to college, this did not affect our relationship with my father's first family. These older brothers and sisters had gone to work in the mines or had married men who did. Even so, the relationship to my father's first family was excellent. We would visit one another often and share our interests and thoughts even though they were older. They would always take time to talk and coach me along the way. My mother was accepted by all of my older brothers and sisters. We were one big family of 13 children. If one of us had a problem and needed assistance, we all would pitch in to help. Of course, some of my nieces and nephews were the same age as me, and I was hardly in an uncle relationship with them. Denver Woolum, my nephew, was one of my best friends. During our spare time, we were always together.

On a typical day, we ate biscuits and gravy plus country ham and eggs for breakfast, soup beans and corn bread, fried chicken, shuck beans, fried apple pies for noon and evening meals most of the time. For Wednesday's noon meal, we would usually have soup beans, scallop potatoes, cornbread, and buttermilk. Much of what we ate was raised or grown on the farm. In this way, my parents extended the family income.

As you might imagine, I don't ever remember going to a restaurant with my parents, but I did go to a restaurant with Virgil in about 1939. It was the original restaurant that Col. Sanders of future Kentucky Fried Chicken (KFC) fame had built two years earlier. Virgil and the rest of the family marveled at how good the chicken tasted. I got to thinking that we had fried chicken at least once a week. We'd sometimes eat a young chicken that I'd run down for my mother and chop its head off with an ax or hatchet. My mother would prepare it well but it didn't taste like KFC.

While Virgil and Pauline worked their way through school, driving that Ford, I made my way through grade school and eventually high school. Those years flew by. Between the farm.

CHAPTER 3

Personal Choices

On September 16, 1940, the U.S. Congress instituted the Selective Training and Service Act, which required all men between the ages of 21 and 45 to register for military service. This was the first peacetime draft in United States' history, and we knew it might affect Virgil at some point. In the fall of my last year of grade school, although World War II had seemed imminent, it was a shocking surprise when the Japanese bombed Pearl Harbor on December 7, 1941. After this savage attack, many older boys who were in their junior and senior year of high school entered the military to assist in the defeat of Germany and Japan.

Virgil registered for the draft, and one week before his number was called to report for active duty, he enlisted in the US Army Air Force, took basic training, completed communication technical course and was reassigned to an Active Duty Unit. During this period, he applied for officer's training school (OTS), completed this course and was appointed a 2nd Lieutenant and spent most of the war years in Peru, South America, as a classified communication officer.

I graduated from grade school in June of 1942 and looked forward to high school. I would be going to a larger school building with many more students.

After a summer of work on the family farm, in the fall of 1942, I entered high school. There was so much that was different. For one thing, my class was made up of students from all over the county and most of us had to be bussed into the centrally located school. As a result, I got to meet young people I had not known before. The high school building, built around 1935 of reddish bricks, had two stories and 10 to 12 rooms. Just that size made it a very different experience from the two-room school building in which I had spent 8 years. In addition, there was also a gym with a basketball court, a cafeteria and a library. It boasted indoor plumbing and a football field behind the building. We seemed to be always changing classes, and when we did so, the wood flooring squeaked beneath our feet. The halls were filled with around 400 students that had been bused from throughout the county. Of those who began with me in 1942, about 50% to 60% graduated.

The quality of teaching varied a lot. It was affected by how much education and training each teacher had received, as well as the teacher's commitment and experience. Unfortunately, some teachers were political appointees who had little training in either teaching or their subject matter. In addition, some student teachers, who were training in their education curriculum, did not have much to offer. I learned early in high school that I had to work extra hard in my studies because of both the low quality of my preparation in primary school and the inadequacy of some of my high-school teachers who were not equipped to help me. To be fair, there were other teachers who did an excellent job of using traditional lectures and discussions. They knew how to encourage and motivate students.

There were no electives offered, and students took identical subjects like English, basic Math, History and several other liberal arts courses. These were subjects that I was not particularly interested in studying. They were required subjects but I rapidly adjusted my study habits to meet these requirements. Unfortunately, we did not have the opportunity to study advanced courses in science, physics or chemistry because they were not available. I feel that I lost out because I had always been interested in these subjects and I think I could have excelled in them.

The high school did not have softball or a baseball team; as a result, I lost momentum and desire for these sports in which I had previously excelled. Instead, I started playing basketball and did this for the next four years. Because of my size, I did not play football but was the manager of the football team during my senior year.

I made friends easily with both boys and girls, some of whom became girlfriends. There were three girls who would contact me during class break and during lunch just to flirt and talk. Wherever I went on campus, they would follow, laugh and flirt. I didn't have time for that because I had arranged to attend all my classes in the morning, (7:30 AM to 12:00 PM) with lunch break lasting until 1:00 PM and then three hours in the afternoon for basketball practice. I had not scheduled any in-school study periods. After practice, I went home on the school bus. The only time I had to talk to these three girls was during class breaks and doing so prevented me from getting to my follow-on classes on time. I wasn't expected nor did I want to get married at a young age as I sensed that I had a bright future ahead of me. This was my primary focus.

As for discipline, even large teens were taken into the principal's office and strapped on the rear with a leather belt while bending over the principal's desk. The strapping was heard about six to eight classrooms down the hall from the principal's office. Everything became really quiet after that.

When students got into trouble at school, they also got into trouble at home. Usually, they would get the same discipline at home. Children were not allowed to get away with mischief and misbehavior in those days. It's too bad that these principles seem to be disappearing today.

During these years, I enjoyed hunting. Most of the time I would go by myself. If two or more guys are walking in the woods, the noise of the leaves and brush under their feet would frighten animals who would run. I like to hunt squirrels and rabbits. Squirrels usually ran up the trees, and it was hard for them to escape unless there were a lot of tree branches nearby. Rabbits hid in the bushes to escape being seen. In 1947, I went on a squirrel-hunting trip with a cousin in Red Bird, Kentucky. We did a lot of walking but did not see any squirrels, of course, because we were making such noise while walking along the route!

Red Bird was where most of my mother's family lived and where she lived during her early years. It was a rural area about 17 miles from Jenson. All of my relatives were hard workers who made their living by farming. I don't think that anyone attended college—much less graduated from one, but they were honest and trustworthy individuals.

During the war and a short period afterwards, we were under federal rationing which included food, gas, as well as many other items. Most people had little discretionary money to spend because what they had was devoted to family necessities and the war effort.

At the end of World War II, the United States emerged as the world's leading industrial power and continues to be so to this day. The economy in Kentucky and the nation expanded and people started to have more disposable income and enjoyed greater material comfort than their parents.

This advantage, along with our education, were the major factors that permitted my siblings and I to accomplish above and beyond what my parents were able to do in their lifetime.

Racing, breeding and riding horses had always been part of the cultural fabrics of Kentucky and after World War II, became even more so as the culture of Kentucky grew more "easy going" and folks could afford more "leisure activities," Outdoor recreation and Bourbon Whiskey, as well as horse racing and horse breeding became a way of life.

Perhaps it was during these high school years, as I was growing up on the farm in Jenson, that I grasped how hard my father and mother were working each day in the house and in the fields. Their work never ended. It began early in the morning and ended late in the evening, and the next day was the same routine. As I grew toward adulthood, I realized that I might succumb to following in their footsteps and that my life risked being as hard as theirs. My parents taught me to work hard, exercise grit, be honest, persevere at any task I undertook and excel according to my ability. For these remarkable character traits, I will always be grateful. I realized that I did not want to spend my days on a hill farm, eking out a hardscrabble life.

My parents had a part in encouraging me to persevere in seeking an education. They would always say, "Get an education so you can make excellent decisions." As long as I completed my assigned chores—remember: we lived essentially in a hand-to-mouth situation and it would not have taken much for us to slip into an even harder life—my parents would support me if I had to write articles in a school newspaper, attend school events, or participate in school debates. The reality of our lives was that we lived

Mother, Christine, Everett, circa 1941

on a farm where we grew our food. There are only 24 hours in a day; the animal had to be fed, cows milked and watered, the gardens tended to. My father was 67 years old when I was born and my mother 37. By the time I was in high school, my father was in his eighties, not as strong as he had once been, and my mother was in her early-fifties. Both Virgil and Pauline were gone—my brother was serving in the military and my sister was either in college or teaching away. That left me and Christine to help with the farm chores, our parents needed our help to manage a farm. As I have already written, when I was growing up, my spare time—we did not have a radio to listen to or a TV to watch—was spent chopping weeds, hoeing corn, plowing, milking, splitting wood. This part of life had to be maintained for the other part—going to school—to happen.

In spite of the deficiency of my early schooling, I managed to keep myself motivated. As I advanced through high school, I felt that I could not let my two older siblings outdo me. I kept plugging along, doing the best I could under the circumstances. My desire has always been to do the best I could at any task. I succeeded at this, as a result I finished number one in my class of 100 students and graduated as valedictorian. Granted it was a small class in a small school, but my ranking revealed to me that I could have more of a life than had been available to my parents.

In retrospect, I know that both my parents' encouragement and the examples of Virgil and Pauline played a major role in inspiring me to do well in high school and attain more than was available in Jenson. It would be a while, however, before I could take up the next phase of my education and achieve the success I aspired to in life.

After finishing high school, I worked at odd jobs to earn spending money and little more. At 17, I contemplated how to continue my education which I could not then afford nor fund. Even though I had a promise of scholarships from three colleges, I did not have a means of transportation to visit those colleges to investigate their offers. Union College was close, but I did not get an offer from Union and I did not have a desire to go there because the school only offered a degree in Education. Both Virgil and Pauline had attended Union College, studied education, and were now teaching. In any case, becoming a teacher was not something I wanted to do.

I was interested in science, math and medicine, but I could not see how to get the education I would need. Meanwhile, with no real jobs to be found in or around Jenson, I was working for 50 cents per day repairing fences and/ or driving trucks, when available. I was on the "bottom rung of the ladder" contemplating my next move which was not, as yet, obvious. In my off time, I built a rock cellar under my parent's cottage, to allow the family to store vegetables for later use. I felt trapped, and I could not see my way out of my dilemma.

The December after my graduation, my father died at age 84, leaving my mother with one dependent child still at home, my sister Christine who was still in high school. Fortunately, I was already working and bringing home some income—however minimal. My father had been active until his death and he and I were working together two weeks before his passing. As long as he could walk, he was doing some type of constructive work. My mother was, of course much younger, and after my father passed, she remained active and continued to do the garden and inside housework. The only available work in Jenson, at that time, was farming and coal mining. Since coal mining was not suitable for my mother, she supported herself and the rest of the family by growing food on the farm. My father left a small amount of money when he died but not enough to sustain a normal lifestyle for any length of time. Since neither my mother or my father had worked at jobs on the outside, in which they might have contributed to Social Security, neither drew funds from the system nor did they have a retirement income. My mother never remarried as there were no men available to date. Within a short-time my mother had a stroke, was paralyzed on her left side, and remained in a retirement home until her death from leukemia on May 25, 1966.

In addition to being there for my mother and my sister when my father died, it was fortunate in a way that I hung around because in January and February 1947, Kentucky was flooded with a major flood. Before the rains started, I was invited to visit my aunt Cellar who lived in Red Bird, my mother's home town, for a few days to sort out my immediate future. After I left home, it rained continuously for three days. There was so much water falling on Kentucky that the rivers could not drain the rainfall fast enough to prevent flooding. One day, my brother Willie and other members of my family came to our home and insisted that my mother and Christine get out of the house and onto higher grounds before the water could wash it away—

which it soon did. A mammoth force of excess water swept our log cabin off its foundation and lodged it against a cherry tree about 50 yards away. Much of it along with most of our possessions were destroyed. Before the flood we had little and now we had less. When the water receded and I returned home from Red Bird, we made a damage assessment. My mother wanted her home rebuilt in its original position. With some outside help, I did just that and raised the foundation above floodwater level.

This time, after both my father's death and the major flood, was a stressful period for the Woolum family. We limped along without making headway. On February 27, I turned 18 without much of a future awaiting me in Kentucky. I had a high school education, but that did not qualify me for much. The difficulty of that time, however, was fortunate in a way for me as it was a turning point in how I envisioned my future. I realized afterwards that I could only depend upon myself and God for future support.

Change would come, but not for over a year and half. In the spring of 1948, realizing there was no meaningful work in that area, I followed Virgil's example and joined the US Air Force. Christine was still in High School, Pauline continued teaching English but I did not want to teach. When I left for the Air Force, she was teaching at Bell County High School, Pineville, Kentucky.

Everett, circa 1949

At the end of the war, Virgil, had been selected to serve as a regular officer which allowed him to remain in service. He had accepted this offer to remain on active duty. By 1948, he had advanced rapidly in the military ranks, and I understood that he had a much better future than I could have if I remained in Kentucky. This is what I wanted for myself, a better future.

CHAPTER 4

Expanding Horizons

Before entering the Air Force and at Virgil's prompting, I had made sure to get a contract with the military to be assigned, after passing the physical and mental exams and completing basic training, to attend Weather Observation School.

I was sworn into the U.S. Air Force on September 10, 1948, and started my basic training at Lackland Air Force Base, San Antonio, Texas.

After basic training, I was promoted to the rank of Private First Class, and I left Texas to start my career in weather by attending and completing the "Weather Observer Course" at Chanute, Air Force Base, in Rantoul, Illinois. We learned to observe and record weather conditions for use in weather forecasting, to take hourly weather observations then transmit this data via teletype machines to be distributed worldwide. In addition, we learned to record data from various sources—thermometers, barometers, hygrometers, humidity, wind velocity and precipitation.

Everett at Chanute, weather school

(arrow points to my quarters)

After completing this course, I was assigned as an observer to Memphis Air Force Station, Tennessee. I really liked being a weather observer and wanting to start my upward advancement; I applied for Rawinsonde Operator School, which was also located at Chanute Air Force Base, in Illinois. After completing this course, I was sent back to the Midwest.

As a graduate of the Rawinsonde Operator School, I would be responsible for collecting upper air data. In those days, we released a helium balloon that ascended to as high as 100,000 feet. A radio transmitter was attached to the balloon and would transmit relevant weather data back to earth.

After this assignment, I was sent to the Pan Handle of Florida to Hurlburt Airfield, where General Doolittle prepared for his flight to raid Tokyo. I only stayed at this location for about three months releasing atmospheric weather balloons.

While I was away from my mother and sister, I had not deserted them in my quest for a better life. My absence was beneficial for them in the long run as I sent them an allotment of $50.00/month which was extracted from my salary of $75.00/month. They were able to live reasonably well on this and my mother was relieved to get the money—I know this is what my father would have wanted me to do. In the meantime, I was developing a career and working for a future retirement. I finally felt that I was making headway in my life and had put behind me the feeling of stagnation

Everett on Maneuvers, Alaska, 1950

that I felt when I was doing menial, odd jobs in Jenson.

After graduating, I was transferred to Alaska where I would spend the next one and a half years performing these tasks. Interestingly while there, during the years of the Korean War, I helped support the Army's test program by actually wearing the cold-weather clothing that was to be used by combat soldiers in the war. We also tested equipment used in, other, extreme low temperature environments (around -50 degrees Fahrenheit). For part of my Alaska tour, I was assigned to Umnak Island, Cape Air Force Base, where my function was to release helium balloons to observe the upper atmosphere. Cape Air Force Base was located at the end of the Aleutian Island chain, near Russia. At times during the winter on Umnak Island, the snow was so abundant that it would pile to the eves of the buildings, keeping us inside until the snow melted or until we had an opportunity to remove enough to escape. The extreme weather made it difficult to receive shipments, as a result, we only received mail once a month.

On a positive note, fishing was great in the area near Fairbanks. We had to walk about 5 miles inland to get to a lake where the fishing was excellent. If we wanted to stay the night, we would bring sleeping bags, but even in warm weather, we had to cut branches and gather dead wood to make a platform under our sleeping bags for protection from the cold ground.

Everett and friends testing cold-weather-gear, 1950

I had petitioned my U.S. Representative for an appointment to West Point, the army's military academy. Unfortunately— in late 1950 or early 1951, while stationed at Umnak Island, I received a letter from my Representative (in our once-a-month mail delivery) informing me that I was two days too old for an appointment! This failure was a disappointing setback in my career plans. Since I was in the Air Force, stationed overseas at that time, I decided to request an assignment to a base close to Texas A&M Military college. I was successful in getting assigned to Bryan Air Force Base, Texas, near College Station and adjacent to Texas A&M. While there, I was able to complete one year of my freshman courses before being transferred.

At this point, I had secured a number of promotions. In August of 1950, at age 21.5, I was promoted to Sargent. The following year in December, I became a Staff Sargent. Then, the next August, I was promoted to Technical Sargent. I was twenty-four. These promotions in rank not only increased my salary but also were an expression of the confidence the Air Force had in me.

After Bryan Air Force Base, I was sent to the Pan Handle of Florida to the airfield where General Doolittle prepared for his flight to raid Tokyo. I only stayed at this location for about three months releasing atmospheric weather balloons.

The next assignment was to Barksdale Air Force Base, Shreveport, Louisiana. After working at this location for about six months I decided to apply for Weather Analysis School.

In 1952, I was accepted for the Weather Analysis Course. This brought me back to Chanute Air Force Base, Rantoul, Illinois, for an additional nine months. I was already familiar with Chanute from having done my training for weather observer and operator there in 1949. This Weather Analysis course was a prep course for Weather Forecasting. We studied how to analyze hemispheric weather maps as well as surface and upper air charts for geographical locations at specific times. These charts were analyzed at 12-hour increments and included surface, 850 MB, 700 MB, 500 MB and 300 MB charts. The MB numbers represent different altitudes in the atmosphere.

We studied a variety of college–level subjects—math (algebra, calculus etc.), thermodynamics, physics, physical science, computer application and environmental science—in order to properly execute both analysis and forecasts. We had to master the drawing of isobars (lines of equal pressure) on surface maps for the entire Northern Hemisphere. Then, we drew contour maps for the same area to get complete pictures of the upper atmosphere. In addition to this intense class and homework assignments, we had to participate in the normal military activities and parades each Saturday, plus open rank inspections on Saturdays too. Of course, it helped that we had GI parties each Friday night! In spite of the intensity of this program, I adjusted to its routine very well and felt positive about my life.

Finally, in November 1952, I graduated from this course, and was ready to work as a weather forecaster. The Air Force transferred me to Bryan Air Force Base, in Bryan, Texas, where I worked in this specialty. Apparently, I did well and the Air Force deemed me a worthy candidate to invest in more weather schooling. They transferred me back to Chanute Air Force Base, in 1953 for the advance Weather Forecaster School. I was on a roll!

The Weather Forecaster School was a nine months course which included similar material as the Weather Analysis course but more intense. The students were expected to have a good command of algebra, physics, calculus and various sciences. These were prerequisites without which we could not succeed in the program. During the first days of class, students were told that 54% of us would not finish the course. presumably, this was said to inspire us to study hard. I took their advice because I did not want to be sent back to my previous base in disgrace, but also because I was not afraid to work as hard, and as smart as necessary to be successful. I had known what it was like to live on a hardscrabble farm where the work was constant and monotonous, where no-work meant no-food. My father's example of working hard into his eighty-fourth year was also before me, as were the lesson of the 1947 flood and the reconstruction of our home afterwards. These experiences taught me to do what it takes to succeed. The instructors at the Weather Forecaster School did well to remind us of the difficulty ahead but they did not need to remind me to access my grit. I did that naturally.

This advanced course included meteorology of the earth's atmosphere and its climate conditions. These subjects were necessary to accurately forecast the weather for particular locations and regions. We learned about worldwide weather stations and how they contribute to the accuracy of the whole picture, about satellite data, radar and remote sensors. Military forecasts have to be more exact than National Weather Service forecasts because aviation safety depends upon it. We had to forecast the bases and tops of clouds for specific locations in the country and abroad. These forecasts alerted pilots whether the weather called for visual flight rules (VFR) or instrument flight rules (IFR). I completed this course in 1954 and returned to Bryan Air Force Base, Texas, to help provide weather forecasting for student navigation.

Having finished my training at Chanute, I was launched on my long career as a meteorologist. From being an oddjobber and occasional truck driver in Jenson, I had at 25, acceded the ranks of a professional. My focus and hard work had paid off. I was confident using a variety of scientific techniques to understand, interpret, observe and predict the earth's atmosphere and its phenomena. It felt great to have this knowledge and to be such an integral part of Air Force aviation and operations.

In the Air Force, I not only learned to be professional but also to be a bigger person. While growing up in Jenson, I very seldom saw an African-American. The only time I saw one was when we went to the nearby small town of Pineville. When I was young, black folks were separated from the whites. They had a separate waiting room in a bus station and they drank water from a separate fountain elsewhere in the building. By the mid-1950, the military was assigning African-American males to reside in the same barracks and to use the same restrooms as whites. Since I had been accustomed to racial separation since childhood, it seemed at first very odd to be living in the same building with an African-American man. Over time I became used to seeing blacks next to me and to not think anything about it. They are like everyone else, good and honest people looking to have a loving marriage and a happy family, chasing their dreams and wanting to develop good careers.

Growing up in Jenson, I was sheltered. I did not know any immigrants who did not speak English. In the Air Force, I met men whose native languages were not English and who sometimes spoke to each other in foreign languages. I had grown up in a community where everyone was Protestant and to be rubbing elbows with Catholics and Jews was a new—and broadening—experience.

While growing up, I only knew small towns and small community cultures. I had never even visited Louisville. Now I was living on military bases near large cities that were centers of commerce and innovation, inhabited by a mix of cultures.

All of this was part of the wonderful education I was receiving while on active duty. While simultaneously helping to defend our country, taking additional college courses, and perfecting an excellent career with the US Air Force. I felt blessed to have such a rich and wonderful life.

CHAPTER 5

My World

Although my focus had been on shaping and developing my career within the Air Force, as serendipity would have it, my new assignment to Bryan Air Force Base, Texas was to lead me in a different direction that would change my life forever. In this, I was a lucky man.

The secretary to the Operation Officer at the base was a young woman named Mary Ann Moore Bell. She recorded each pilot's flight hours on a daily basis. We crossed paths and found ourselves talking to each other frequently. Among the first things I noticed about Mary Ann was that she was down to earth, unselfish, patient and understanding. She had good traditional values—Christian values—and an excellent personality. Mary Ann grew up in a small Texas town about 100 miles south of Dallas; her father was a farmer and later worked as an electrician. She came from a modest background that taught her to work hard and to plan for the future. From the beginning, I found her cute and charming but her personality and sensible clothes impressed me the most. This went on until it was obvious, we wanted to date each other. We became very good friends and eventually decided to marry. Comparing her to the few other women that I dated, she out shined them all. Our wedding occurred on October 10, 1956, in Bryan, Texas, approximately one year after we met. We

Our Wedding, 1956

both had similar goals and expectations for our life together and our vision was tested, and proven accurate by our successful 32 years of marriage, prior to Mary Ann's passing in 1988.

Mary Ann had a daughter, Brenda, from a previous marriage, and since we took to each other right away, it was easy for us to form a new family. Mary Ann proved to be an excellent military wife, an extrovert with an excellent personality, and would make friends easily when we moved to a new assignment. She never complained about loneliness during the many times when I was absent from home on maneuvers or exercises. We were a well-matched couple who enjoyed each other's company. It helped a lot that we had the same goals in life. Mary Ann was honest, responsible, loving and supportive. I was lucky to find a mate with these attributes.

Soon after we married, I was transferred to Kindley Air Force Base, in Bermuda to work in the Atlantic Forecast Center. The first home we had in Bermuda was a converted barn. There were no quarters available on base so we had no other choice but to find living accommodations as we could. Our family lived on the upper part of the barn since the building was built on an incline or slope. Another family, the Harvey's, lived in the lower part. Our apartment consisted of two bedrooms with modern conveniences, but it was nothing fancy. Because the island had little fresh water, we had to collect our water from the flow of rain off the roof to a tank below. We lived there for about a year and then moved to a nice three-bedroom home closer to the Air Force Base. Our new home was sparsely but sufficiently furnished to live in comfortably. Our Bermuda assignment provided great memories since this was our first assignment together, as newlyweds.

At Kindley Air Force Base, I was on a team that provided weather support for US Military in the North Atlantic Region. Additionally, we supported the British Airways flights departing Bermuda. Since the base was very busy, we had the opportunity to participate in varied activities.

Very soon after arriving on the island, on 9 November 1956, after I briefed members of a Martin Marlin aircraft, it took off with ten crewmen on board. The aircraft crashed 400 miles north of Bermuda where it disappeared in the Atlantic—one of hundreds and possibly thousands of aircraft and ships to disappear in the Bermuda Triangle. Just in the fifteen years since the base opened in 1941, there had been at least a half dozen disappearances of American aircraft.

We once helped save a large military dirigible balloon when it could not land because of high surface winds. High winds are a tremendous problem when a large balloon is attempting to land. The pilot of this particular balloon was attempting to land with surface winds of 35 knots, gusting to 50. The crew threw ropes down close enough to the earth for people—me among them—to catch. We assembled as many men as were available, to help in this effort. We finally brought this balloon to the runway.

Mary Ann worked as a secretary for the three and half years while we were stationed in Bermuda. Our family explored the island about every week, and took many pictures of this lovely place. When we stayed closer to home, we enjoyed swimming and many of the excellent outdoor activities. I continued to take college courses and learned car mechanics, as time permitted. While stationed in Bermuda, the family took a vacation to New York City. We saw some of the major attractions, such as Radio City Music Hall, the Statue of Liberty, Wall Street and much more. This was a memorable visit.

The island had limited water resources so we learned to conserve water. At home, our system for catching rainwater hitting the roof sometimes failed. When there was a prolonged dry spell and the water was low in the tank, we fetched water in buckets and pails from the Air Force Base.

When President Eisenhower visited Bermuda for a conference with Prime Minister McMillan of Great Britain in March 1957, I had the honor of being in a group of military staff that greeted him at the base.

In the spring of 1961, I was transferred from Bermuda to James Connally Air Force Base, in Waco, Texas. This would place Mary Ann closer to her family. Our daughter Brenda Sue who had been born on December 3, 1950, was ten and had been away from her maternal grandparents for four years. Mary Ann's parents were now able to get to know her again and Brenda to know them. This made the Moore's very happy. Our son, Jerry Dean, was born on April 19, 1962[1], and so was eleven and a half years younger than his sister. After his birth we felt our family was complete.

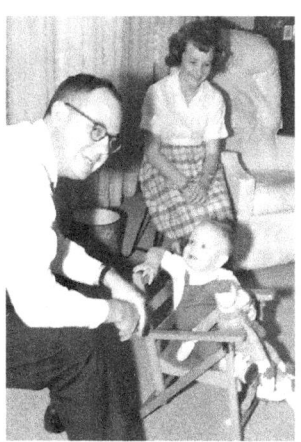

Happy family, circa 1963

---

1   Before Jerry's birth, Mary Ann had a miscarriage

Now that we had our two children—Brenda and Jerry, Mary Ann stayed home to care for the kids and to keep the home fires burning while I was away. A few years later, she obtained a sales job working part time for the Avon cosmetic company, just to make a few bucks for personal spending. From the beginning, Jerry was very active. A couple of days after birth, he could turn over in bed. He continued that hyper-activity as he went through the terrible two's and seemed to get into everything. Mary Ann often

On the way to Church, 1964

found herself to be the parent in charge as I was quite often away on temporary duty. Working night shift and/or performing the many military tasks that were required of me. Since I was on call as a weather forecaster, I was called away from home often to work all types of military exercises. During these constant and unforeseeable periods, Mary Ann was always ready to take up any task related to family affairs and personal activities that I could no longer do. She was not hesitant to make needed decisions. Again, she proved to be an ideal military wife.

Our home at James Connally Air Force Base, Texas, was base quarters, across the street from a Major General who was in charge of the 2nd Air Force, Air Training Command. It was a three-bedroom home, large enough to accommodate our small family very well and was furnished by the US Air Force. It was very close to where I worked and I could walk to work, if I chose.

James Connally Air Force Base was set up to provide navigator training under the Air Training Command, and my assignment was to provide accurate and detailed weather briefing for the navigation training program. This work, was always crucial for the safety of the aircrews. The workload became even more intense after I was appointed chief weather forecaster, which placed me in charge a number of forecasters and analysts. This was an encouraging promotion as it recognized my professionalism, knowledge and leadership. At the time I was a Senior Master Sergeant (SMSgt).

In October 1962, my second year at James Connally Air Training Command, things got more dramatic when U-2 spy-planes, flying over Cuba, detected that the island nation held Soviet nuclear-tipped missiles. President John F. Kennedy was briefed on this information, and with his cabinet, decided to demand the withdrawal of the missiles. What ensued was known as the Cuban Missile Crisis. Two armored divisions from Fort Hood, Texas, were then scheduled to be transferred to Florida for a possible invasion of Cuba. My weather briefings informed this transfer. Fortunately, the invasion was never carried-out as the Soviets backed down, and the men of the divisions were not placed in harm's way.

Always eager to continue my education, I took correspondence courses via US Mail; I also attended the non-commissioned officer's training school at Orlando, Florida. This non-commissioned officer's course was 3 month long, and it was a pre-requisite course for the promotion to Chief Master Sargent (CMSgt). Since Mary Ann did not accompany me, this assignment placed her in charge of the kids without my help. She was a jewel.

In the mid-1960s, Mary Ann was constantly fainting, doing so many times each day. When I would go for work, I did not know that I would see her alive when I arrived home. Many times, she would collapse on the floor during an episode, and Jerry, who was a toddler, would try to entice her to get up by hitting her with cooking pans. Obviously, something had to be done. When her doctor recommended a pacemaker, we were relieved to know there might be an end to the fainting. The procedure was accomplished in a Ft Worth, TX civilian hospital. Mary Ann's mother came and stayed with the children for few days during the pacemaker operation and remained with Mary Ann for a few weeks during her recuperation period. Fortunately, the pacemaker corrected the constant fainting caused by the lack of blood to Mary Ann's brain. After the operation, she did very well for a period of 10 years. During that time, my work continued as always.

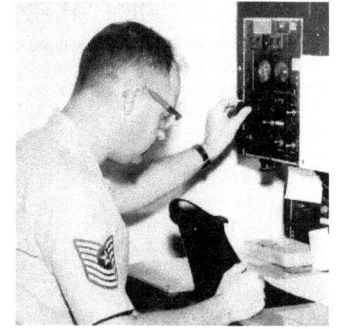

Everett working the weather radar

On one occasion in the mid-60's, I vectored President Johnson and his pilot around a severe thunderstorm, by referencing the Base's Weather Radar. It was a great honor to be responsible for the air safety of our President.

In February 1966, I turned 37 and had been in the military for 17 years. I was living a life I enjoyed and had a lovely family. Brenda was fifteen and Jerry was almost four. That spring, I learned that I was to be transferred to a base in Hawaii. By the end of May, Mary Ann and I were in the process of going to the West Coast in order to transit to Hawaii. When we reached Phoenix, Arizona, in late May, a bit of sadness came into my life as I learned that, on May 25, 1966, my mother had died at age 73. Unfortunately, I was on my way to my next assignment at Wheeler Air Force Base, Hawaii, and could not attend her funeral because the Oakland, California, Port Authority would not delay the departure date assigned for going overseas.

This filled me with a great sadness because it would have been appropriate for me to pay my last respect to my wonderful mother. Even though she had had a humble beginning and a hard road in life, she taught me many things, from my birth to my early adulthood when I left home: to respect other people, to be honest, to work hard and to succeed in life.

I arrived at Wheeler Airfield, located only 20 miles from Honolulu on Oahu Island, which had been a primary target of the first Japanese attack on 7 December 1941. By 1966, the assault was a distant memory, and the base was fully functional. I worked in the Pacific Forecast Center, located underground in a mountain of Hawaii. This was still during the Cold War, and so, to be protected from an atomic bomb, the headquarters were positioned underground in a mountain.

The Headquarters building was a large, 3 levels structure inside a mountain. We had to walk through a tunnel for a quarter mile or more, pass several gates and guards. We also entered codes at several point before arriving at our duty station. Our unit was on the 3rd level. Our responsibility was to brief the Pacific Command Headquarters of weather activities involving the Vietnam War plus any adverse weather activity elsewhere in the Pacific. You have to remember that we were still involved in the Cold War and this underground facility was designed to help us to survive an attack and be able to wage war in retaliation. I was dealing with highly classified projects at the time and can't say much more.

I participated in all types of weather analyses whose goal was to support our military in the Vietnam War. The Pacific Command's responsibility encompasses more than 100 million square miles (260,000,000 km2), or roughly 52 percent of the Earth's surface, stretching from the waters off the West Coast of the United States west coast of India and from the Arctic to the Antarctic. During this period, I was not in charge of any personnel. My primary job was to brief pilots and crewmembers of weather conditions from Hawaii and throughout the Pacific to Vietnam. I was a SMSgt at the time.

After I had been there one year, the Pacific Command Headquarters was transferred to Hickam Air Force Base in Honolulu, and I was moved along with this group. This was a nice move since instead of being underground, now I had a window. My duties at Hickam Air Force Base, were again to brief pilots and analyze maps. Later, I was transferred to the section that only briefed F4 and KC135 crews headed for Vietnam, as the war was in high gear then. The work-load was demanding and the weather brief accuracy was crucial to those crews. Almost daily, I would brief 20 F4 and 3 KC135 tankers Crews performing refueling missions enroute to Guam. I briefed these pilots in a separate room rather than in the weather briefing section near the control tower. This arrangement worked better in order to brief the large groups of airmen involved.

This reassignment to Hickam required that the entire family move from Wheeler Air Force Base to Hickam Air Force Base, Hawaii, about 20 miles south on the same island. We were assigned a furnished three-bedroom quarters on Hickam, close to work but with standard GI furnishings… again, nothing special.

While stationed in Hawaii, I was sent to Okinawa on a number of maneuvers with the Army's 82nd Airborne Division. We were to simulate establishing a command post behind "enemy" lines in what was designated as "North Korea." The aircraft were flown from Okinawa close to the actual North Korean border before making a 180-degree turn. The paratroopers would then jump and land in South Korea, near Seoul, thus simulating a jump into enemy territory.

On one particular exercise, the weather over South Korea had become a problem because of high winds associated with a moving cold front. I recommended to the Commanding General to delay the mission 24 hours because of the deteriorating weather and because the surface winds were too strong for airborne troops to land. The General accepted my recommendation as the safety of the men was paramount. Twenty-four hours later at 04:00 AM, I again gave another weather briefing, for schedule departure at 06:00 AM. This time, the winds were within limits for paratroopers to land, so we could proceed with the exercise.

The planes took off and proceeded to the North Korean border where they did not cross over but abruptly returned south. As scheduled, the paratroopers made a safe landing without any casualties, in south-central South Korea. Mission Accomplished! These exercises test our country's readiness to fight a war by giving pilots familiarity with conditions of an attack mission and to provide the paratroopers with an exercise that simulated going into actual combat. The mission also honed our command and communications capabilities and tested the whole process for possible weak points.

The Commanding General would always ask for me to accompany his planned exercises. Additionally, I was alerted to be prepared to leave for Vietnam three times but, as luck would have it, I never had to go. Even though I was not sent to Vietnam, I was constantly prepared to go because military readiness demanded it. In order to be ready for deployment I took all the necessary shots for Southeast Asia and continued to train at the firing range (I was an expert rifleman); also, I was fully briefed on what to expect over there, in case the call came. I never asked to be relieved of this assignment, it just worked out that I was not called to go. Who knows how this Memoir would have read, had things been different?

In 1968, because so many awards were being given to professional athletes, Mary Ann decided I deserved an award also and gave me a "sports" award. She was expressing kindness to me, which was great, and I appreciated her thoughtfulness very much. I guess she calculated I was a "good sport."

In the summer of 1968, the Air Force granted me a sabbatical to attend Chaminade University full time. By 1968, I was within a year of earning a degree, and so I jumped at the opportunity. Graduating from college had been my dream since I was a young man in Jenson. Although I had worked and studied hard, I had not had the opportunity. This offer was my chance of a lifetime, and I eagerly pursued it. How my life has changed since those early years in Kentucky. One has to always be ready to take advantage of an opportunity when it knocks.

The Air Force referred to this educational program as the "Bootstrap Program." This allows members of the armed forces the opportunity to complete their college education while on active duty. I was allotted one-year to complete my degree. Chaminade University, a Catholic-affiliated, four-year college that was later to receive the designation of University, was located in a residential neighborhood approximately two miles outside of <u>Waikiki</u> and four miles from <u>down-town Honolulu</u> and proved an ideal location for this opportunity.

Everett, college graduation, 1969

During the two semesters I was in the Bootstrap Program—which was all the time I needed to finish my BA in General Studies with a major focus on Business and English, I received my full wages, tuition, books, and my other related expenses, compliments of the US Military. This was a wonderful period in my life as it permitted me to eliminate the night classes, which had been a staple of my learning for the previous twenty years; I could devote my full energy to my education. I completed my last year of college at Chaminade and received a Bachelor of General Studies in June 1969 with a grade point average of 3.91 out of a possible 4.0. Education has been a lifelong pursuit for me, and I continue learning, now into my 90's.

Everett and Christine, Hawaii, 1969

My sister, Christine, and her husband, Frank, came to my graduation from Chaminade University. While there, we visited the beautiful island of

Oahu and explored many of its famous attractions, USS Arizona Memorial and Diamond Head, etc.

Later that year, I was promoted to Chief Master Sargent (CMSgt). Chief Master Sargent is the ninth, and highest, enlisted rank in the U.S. Air Force, just above Senior Master Sergeant, and is a senior non-commissioned officer rank. The official term is "Chief Master Sergeant" or "Chief".

I have often wondered, what my life would have been like if I had been accepted to West Point and completed the schooling. I would have graduated in 1956 or 1957, been sent to Vietnam, many other dangerous overseas assignments and only God knows what would have happened to me. On the flip side, I could possibly have been promoted to a General and been in charge of several thousand men.

In retrospect, "what could have been" is not important to me. "what can be" is a much more important thought, always look to the future. Things have played out reasonably well in my life. I had a successful marriage and lovely kids. I have been successful in my many choices so far. I've reached the age of 96, and I'm currently planning my next nine years. All in all, I can say that I am very content with my Life.

Very soon after graduating from Chaminade, I was appointed to participate in the first US moon landing and its return trip. Both the US and the USSR had done "hard moon landings"—that is, landings that were lunar crashes without the possibility of a return. NASA had been intent for a number of years to pull off a moon landing and return to earth in a race against the former Soviet Union which had upstaged the US on several occasions. As flight follower, I was charged with monitoring weather conditions for the Neil Armstrong-Buzz Aldrin departure on July 16, 1969.

Our information was fed to both the astronauts and the Command Post. My flight-following responsibilities pertained only within the earth's atmosphere and not outer space for which I did not have data or knowledge. Other specialists who knew all about radio waves, sun flares, and other issues that could cause flight problems handled the outer space details.

The landing on July 20 was very successful and the astronauts executed their maneuvers to return to earth. Although I had first provided the mission with departure information that showed fairly routine weather, as the mission got closer to the July 24 return date—I detected a serious weather threat to the landing. While Neil Armstrong and his co-pilot, Buzz Aldrin, were still on the moon, I discovered an easterly wave—a meteorological term for a storm—developing in the South Pacific Ocean, near their designated splash down area. This storm had a potential of twenty-foot surface waves at the mission's destination landing. Since twenty-foot waves are too high for a safe landing, I informed the Command Post of this potential threat. Command Post took my advice seriously and adjusted the flight to move the splash down location 200 miles to the north. As a result, Neil Armstrong and Buzz Aldrin landed safely on July 24, 1969, in the South Pacific Ocean with only eight-foot surface waves. This was within tolerance for a safe landing.

NATIONAL AERONAUTICS AND SPACE ADMINISTRATION
MANNED SPACECRAFT CENTER
HOUSTON, TEXAS 77058

IN REPLY REFER TO: CB

AUG 2 9 1969

1st Lt Robert J. Armstrong
c/o Det 4 1st Wea Wg
Hickam AFB, Hawaii 96553

Dear Lt Armstrong:

Thank you very much for your kind letter of congratula-
tions on Apollo XI. We certainly appreciate the fine
weather you were able to conjure for us in the alternate
landing area. Please convey our sincere thanks to the
members of your organization for their fine work in the
Pacific.

I am enclosing the official Apollo XI patch which you
requested. Its distribution is limited to those who
have directly contributed to the success of our program.
We will be pleased to have our patch added to that of
the many fine organizations that are included on your
board.

Best wishes.

Sincerely,

Neil A. Armstrong

Enclosure

Appreciation Letter from Neil Armstrong, first man to land on the Moon.

From a farm boy in Kentucky, I had become a serious professional who
had helped execute a historic event. The thrill of that personal realization was
enhanced by the award of an Air Force Commendation Medal for meritorious
service from 1966 to 1969, to include my work on the Moon Landing Mission.

I had come a long way from Jenson, Kentucky!

CHAPTER 6

Wrapping Things Up

By 1969 I could have retired, as I had reached the 20-year mark in the military, but I felt that this wasn't the proper time to do so. I did not have a graduate degree, had not reached the top salary grade to qualify for an excellent retirement pension, and my life savings was not as high as I would have liked. In addition to this, my wife was gravely and chronically ill. The military doctors available to us were excellent. With all the medial problems Mary Ann had, we had to think very hard about exiting the military knowing that, once we were out of the Air Force, this constant quality care she was receiving would not be as easily accessible. Living on base as we were, the hospital was a short drive away, but once we would have moved off-base, getting to the hospital would require a longer drive. We also had to keep in mind that active-duty people and their families had priority on appointments to be seen by a doctor and on hospital procedures. Retirement would have put us—Mary Ann crucially—in a lower priority and so we decided to postpone my retirement for a while.

While not yet ready to retire, plans of doing so at some point were in my mind. My brother Virgil who had preceded me in the Air Force had retired. He was in a different situation, however. He already had an Education BA when he entered the service in 1942. This degree permitted him to become an officer a few months later. When he retired as a Lieutenant Colonel, he had twenty-two years of service. After Virgil retired, he attended Texas A&M University and received a second master's degree. Whereas his first graduate degree had been in Safety at New York University, this one was in Education and further prepared him to teach. Eventually, he became a high school principal before retiring from his second profession. Virgil had established a path to a second career, which had led him to a very successful life. I felt that it was important for me to do the same. Mary Ann and I had determined that I should finish college and possibly get a second degree before retiring from the Air Force.

For now, military life offered me much. While some of my experiences were historic like the moon shot, other opportunities were more on the fun side. Late in 1969, I participated in another personal first when I was appointed by my commanding officer to lend my weather expertise for the filming of the movie *"TORA! TORA! TORA!"* The film dramatized the Imperial Japanese Navy attack on Pearl Harbor, in the American Territory of Hawaii, on Sunday morning December 7, 1941. (The word *TORA* means *tiger* in Japanese. As it was used here by the military, it was a code meaning, "Lightening attack was successful." This was an indication to their superiors that the objective had been achieved with complete surprise). President Roosevelt called December 7, 1941, "a date which will live in infamy.[2]"

The Japanese had big plans to control the entire Eastern Pacific Ocean area and many of its perimeter countries—especially the Asian countries. In order to do this, the Japanese assessed they had to prevent the U.S. Pacific Fleet from interfering. Their attack on the large American fleet anchored at Pearl Harbor had been in the planning for months. At the same time, the Japanese were preparing for military action in Southeast Asia against the United Kingdom in Singapore and Hong Kong, the Netherlands in Indonesia and the US in the Philippines.

The attack commenced at 7:48 AM Hawaii time and ended about fifteen minutes later. Three hundred and fifty-three Imperial Japanese aircraft dive bombers and torpedo bombers (Zero aircraft), in two waves launched from six aircraft carriers, attacked Pearl Harbor and Hickam AFB[3]. All eight U.S. Navy battleships in port were damaged; four were sunk. Seven were subsequently raised and put back into service—the USS Arizona, however, was too badly damaged to be rescued. In all, there were 2,403

---

2   I was 12 years old when Japan attacked Pear Harbor. I was stunned and could not comprehend the major damage the Japanese had just inflicted on the US. Since my family did not have radio or TV, the information I received was sparse. Whenever I could have access to a radio, I was glued to it to hear its announcements. Even at that young age, I would have gone to do my part in defeating this enemy. As I grew older and knew more about the conflict, I was sure that the service was my destiny. The war ended in 1945 before I became old enough to join or be drafted

3   Hawaii did not become a State until August 21, 1959.

Americans killed and 1,178 wounded. The U.S. declared war on Japan the next day, and our long struggle to overcome this catastrophe was launched. The war with Japan ended in 1945, only after the U.S. dropped two atomic bombs that destroyed the cities of Nagasaki and Hiroshima.

During the filming, I briefed Japanese-American actor-pilots on weather conditions around the Hawaiian Islands. They were flying American T-6 aircraft that had been modified to look like Japanese Zero aircraft. Of course, while the planes were simulating a Japanese attack, they were in actual flight. To operate safely, the actor-pilots needed accurate weather information just like any other pilot. While some of the movie was filmed around the other Hawaiian Islands, most of it was done on the island of Oahu, where the Japanese attack occurred. After my briefing, I would see the aircraft in the distance flying over the Pacific as they simulated attacks.

An interesting side note: I was filmed several times during the simulated attack, but these clips were not included in the final release. The reason they gave me was they wanted the story to depict a surprise attack and could not show an American military person briefing their pilots.

In 1970, my family and I were transferred to Travis AFB, in Fairfield, California. We said goodbye to friends in Hawaii and shipped our furniture to California. As my family sailed by cruise ship from Honolulu to San Francisco, we realized once again that a big task was before us: to set up home and make a new circle of friends. When we arrived at Travis, they assigned us temporary quarters until permanent housing became available. Since permanent quarters were in high demand, it took several weeks before a family that had been relocated to another base vacated a house that we could use. Most of the time Government quarters were furnished or, at least, partially furnished. On some of the assignments, we had to purchase a few essential items, but the quarters were mostly move-in ready. Much of the furniture we owned had been stored in Texas in 1966. When our furniture arrived from Texas after three and a half years in storage at extreme heat, a lot of damage had occurred. The government reimbursed us for those pieces that were no longer serviceable.

I knew that I would have my work cut out for me at Travis Air Force Base. With its 1,500 aircraft movements per month, it was known to be the busiest passenger and cargo terminal in the United States. I was assigned as Chief Forecaster at Travis, supervising eight weather forecasters, some of whom not only outranked me but also had more experience.

I had known the commander, Lieutenant Colonel Geron during my recently completed assignment in Hawaii. At the time, he was a major. Based on our acquaintance, he felt that I was the person to help him lead the unit. Previous to my assignment, he and I had worked together for nearly three years, playing golf each Wednesday afternoon and making many military decisions together. He had confidence in my ability to supervise personnel whom I outranked. As a result, we did not have any problems with insubordination. We had a job to do and all personnel did their part.

The weather office was busy around-the-clock. The midnight shift analyzed local charts, generated daily forecasts, and prepared longer-term forecasts which involved many applications that took into account laws of physics, laws of science, geographical properties (mountains, oceans, rivers, streams, etc.), satellite data, surface and upper air charts, fronts, tornadoes, typhoons, to name a few. An excellent forecast study may take months to assemble. From that study, the office would generate a "general forecast," a statement saying what the weather will be at a particular time and area. From that, a "specific forecast" is generated which includes, among other things, the temperature, winds, cloud base and tops and the intensity of the precipitation at a specific location. All of this information had to be continually updated and cross-checked in order to give the "end users and decision makers," the pilots and commanders, the important information they required to maintain safe operations.

The overnight staff also prepared weather slides for the all-important morning briefing. With as much experience as I had by then, it took me only a few minutes to check in with the night crew and become familiar with the synoptic situation. Then, at 07:00, I went in for the 5 minutes I was allotted to brief the Commanding General and his staff on any severe weather worldwide that would impact their flight operations for the Military Airlift Command. They were mostly interested in what would immediately prevent them from moving cargo and supplies.

Following this briefing, I went back to my office to prepare schedules for my forecasters and to perform my many administrative duties. We kept at least two or three forecasters busy on each of the three shifts. Whether on day, swing or midnight shifts, our forecasters were assigned heavy workloads, but this was necessary to service all the "users" that depended on us. The weight of the workload also fell on my shoulders as I was ultimately responsible for all the weather products that my forecasters produced.

In addition, I conducted training for Reserve Officers. This consisted of assigning individuals to shifts—day, swing or midnight—so they could perform the same functions as they trained with the active duty officers. This included analyzing charts, briefing pilots, preparing forecasts, transmitting these forecasts via teletype and answering the phone. The Reserve Officers were eager to do their part of this pressing work. As reservists, they trained to maintain proficiency so they could augment the active duty in case of war as they competed with other reservists for promotions. Their reserve duties were in addition to whatever civilian job in which they engaged.

In addition to writing efficiency reports for Reserve US Air Force Officers. I also created, and maintained, the local weather forecast manual which guided the staff. The work seemed to be never ending as our Global Weather never took a break, and was constantly changing, forcing us to keep up 24/7.

Despite the heavy workload at the Travis Air Force Base, I continued my other pursuits. The San Francisco area presented an abundance of educational opportunities. While at Travis, I decided to pursue an MBA degree. Golden Gate University offered a Continuing-Education program which was a convenient way to further my education. I had in mind that I would work in business once I was out of the Air Force and this was a ticket to both credentialing myself and acquiring some experience in business theory. After much effort, I obtained a master's degree in business administration (MBA) in 1973.

The MBA curriculum at Golden Gate University taught leadership skills and business knowledge using an activity-based approach. Faculty members were seasoned professionals in their respective fields and prepared students to be leaders in a complex business environment. We used Harvard University textbooks, major reports and studies, and twice-weekly classes to meet the objectives. My concentration was in management.

While my plan for furthering my education had gone well, it had spanned twenty years and had not been easy. It was difficult for me to juggle my work and class schedule. Most of the time, I had to work the midnight shift in order to have the day free for a class. During that period, I would only get four hours sleep per day. I learned later, that this is not a good practice in order to maintain excellent health. Sustaining this hectic schedule reduced the time I had with my family, but I felt this sacrifice would provide us a better future. I would say that we must all do what we think is right based on the information we have at the time. Looking back now, I don't think I would make any changes.

While at Travis, we enrolled Jerry in a school which was located on base. There wasn't any delay in that regard. Because of the age difference between our two children, we were assigned a three-bedroom house which worked very well. While at Travis, Brenda left for college in Texas and never came back. I had moved permanently or temporarily 21 times during my 26 years of active duty. The moves from base to base affected Brenda more than Jerry. Brenda made friends very easily, but after a few years, she had to leave them. I think that she still corresponds with some of her friends from that time.

Retirement day, 1 Nov 1974

They were military children and were moving around all the time, too.

By the spring of 1974, Mary Ann and I were discussing when I would leave the Air Force. I had twenty-five years plus of service, and I was definitely thinking about embarking on a new career. It was a very difficult decision for my wife and me to make. I could have stayed another four years or longer which would have placed me at thirty years. At the thirty-year mark, I would have been nearly 50 years old with a slimmer chance of getting employed with a civilian company. We decided to exit the service now that I was forty-five and move on to civilian life by the end of the year. At that point, I would have put in a full twenty-six years. When I retired, I ranked in the top 1% of the enlisted grade.

My children grew up in the 1950s and the 1960s. This was a time when great changes took place that helped shape our nation into what it is today. The biggest change came after the Second World War which ended in 1945. Veterans had an opportunity to go to school through the GI Bill and to set goals for a brighter future. When they married, they were able to offer more opportunities to their families. Women's horizons expanded as they joined the workforce and experienced access to more education.

Although the nuclear family is still the most common family type in America, if current television sitcoms teach us anything, it is that the contemporary family structure is not always nuclear. There are now millions of households with different family structures. Recent studies show, however, that the nuclear family is still dominant with about 54% of households in America described as such[4].

The traditional nuclear household, two parents under the same roof as their kids, seems to me to be the ideal family. One parent—usually the father—works to procure income and the other parent—usually the mother—works to maintain a home that everyone can return to. The nuclear family is an elementary family unit according to sociological and anthropological points of view. This sort of nuclear family is what Mary Ann and I created and endeavored to maintain. In this goal, I feel we were successful. I went to work daily for the income our family needed, and Mary Ann made sure there was food in the refrigerator and in the cupboards and she saw to it that the house was clean and pleasant. She also sewed and repaired clothing.

The 1980's saw the end of the dominance of the traditional family unit. Life became more stressful as there were two recessions within a decade. The divorce rates were increasing and this produced more families in which parents did not live together.

---

4   Data taken from https://www.fastcompany.com/3062162/the-nuclear-family-is-still-the-majority-of-us-households-just-barely

In spite of all the family problems within our society, my family bonded, worked hard, planned for the future and appreciated each other's accomplishments, all the credit goes to Mary Ann, who was the glue that kept us together. After her death, it became difficult to maintain that close-knit family structure, especially as the children moved away and began their own families. Such is the current state of affairs in this country.

In preparation for a return to civilian life, Mary Ann and I bought a custom home for $50,000 in Fairfield, California, near Travis AFB. Buying this home made sense because it was near a large military hospital that could care for her medical needs. We fully intended on staying in Fairfield as Travis AFB provided many benefits. As we approached separation, the medical personnel suggested we replace her pacemaker before we depart. Her original pacemaker was installed in the stomach area with leads to the heart. The new pacemaker would be implanted above the breast on the left side with easy access to attach the leads to the heart. This operation was more involved since they were moving the main pacemaker component to the breast area and had to remove the leads in the stomach area. It took her longer to recover, but the operation was a success and provided Mary Ann with a newer and more advanced device.

Before my retirement date arrived, I had three civilian job offers in the field of meteorology. One job offer was at Texas A & M. I was to manage their weather station, teach one course, and complete a PHD. The opportunity to continue furthering my education was appealing. In addition, Mary Ann and I were familiar with the area as I had been stationed there in the fifties. My wife and I made the decision not to take the Texas A&M job because the schedule would have been too hectic, almost impossible. They offered to pay me only $900/month as they thought that since I was getting military retirement pay, the $900 would be sufficient—it wasn't. Knowing I would be near Mary Ann's family if I accepted this job, my father-in-law wanted me to take over managing his farm, 15 miles away. It had one hundred head of cattle. This was a serious offer from my father-in-law. He had been an electrician who had become disabled from a fall. We had the feeling that he wanted to give the farm to Mary Ann, but she had no interest in becoming a farmer's wife, and had no desire to live out in the country[5].

A second offer was for a job as a weather forecaster in Long Beach, California. This would have required a move to the Los Angeles area where the living expenses were very high. In addition, I didn't think that the job was permanent; therefore, we didn't seriously consider it.

The final weather job offer was at a university in Houston, Texas. Since weather goes on twenty-four hours a day, and so must the job of weather analysis. After working shifts for many years, I felt that it was time to find a permanent, non-weather-related job. That meant leaving weather analysis and forecasting behind so none of these jobs appealed to me.

As I prepared to wrap up my twenty-six years with the Air Force, I continued to look for employment outside of weather. About two weeks after Mary Ann's operation, I was offered a job as a financial analyst with Philco Ford in Palo Alto, California. I accepted the offer. Ironically, after spending twenty-six years in the Air Force, I was to spend the next 26 years in the aerospace industry. I joined Philco Ford on October 1, taking advantage of a thirty-day leave that was due me prior to retiring from the Air Force in November 1974, I was able to double-dip and get paid both for my leave and for my work at Philco Ford. The additional money was helpful during the transition.

---

5   Four years after my father-in-law offered me the farm management, my mother-in-law died. Two or three years after that, he decided to come live with us in California. He really enjoyed living here and said he wished he could have come to California when he was a boy. He enjoyed the fruits and vegetables on the California farms and he especially liked the nice weather we had. Mary Ann didn't get the farm but did get a house, which we eventually sold.

Because I did not want to travel from Fairfield to Palo Alto every day, we rented the Fairfield home to an active duty pilot who was the commander of a squadron in Travis AFB. He had just returned from a tour in Vietnam. This was the beginning of my

My Sunnyvale home since March, 1975

real-estate management venture. My wife and I purchased a new home in Sunnyvale, California. I still live in the same home, even though my wife passed away in 1988.

In hindsight, I think that I made the correct decision by choosing a career in the aerospace industry and living in Silicon Valley, the center of technology. This move allowed me to reach my goals to travel, feel settled, invest and enjoy life.

CHAPTER 7

A *"Living" Situation*

S ometimes life "throws you a bone." Although I believe that in many ways, I believe more strongly that we make our own luck through proper planning. Such was the case as Mary Ann and I began our transition to civilian life. There is a saying that "proper prior planning prevents poor performance." I have been a "planner" my entire life. I actively look for daily opportunities to gather, analyze, and plan my future strategy. This constant planning caused me to see the need to save and invest in order to have options. Saving and investing then allowed me to have the resources in place to take advantage of opportunities.

My planning takes many forms: education to keep up with, and understand, future trends and circumstances; attention to finances to have the means to benefit from my education; a spiritual practice to have the clarity of vision that comes from daily conversations with my creator; maintenance of my physical condition to stay in shape and to have the energy to pursue opportunities. All of this takes a lot of work and commitment. Sadly, few people are willing to do what it takes. *"If you keep doing what you've been doing, you'll keep getting what you've been getting."* If you're not happy with your present situation, change something!

My retirement from the Air Force necessitated that I find my own housing. For the previous 26 years, I had bounced between approximately 26 different government housing situations. Starting out at basic training in Texas, I then moved to weather school in Illinois, then to Tennessee, back to Illinois, to Alaska at four different locations, to Florida, to Louisiana, back to Illinois, to Texas, to Bermuda at two different locations, back to Texas, back to Florida, back to Texas for two different assignments, to California, to Hawaii at two locations, back to California at Travis Air Force Base.

We liked Fairfield, and we thought it would be wise to buy a home near the base. This would allow us to make use of the base exchange, its medical hospital, and the many other facilities that we were so familiar with after years in the service. As a result, Mary Ann and I bought our very first house several miles from the front gate of Travis. We had the typical first-time-homebuyer reservations about this purchase: did we have the funds to fall back upon, if things went south? As is usually the case, we thought this would be our "forever house".

By the time we had completed the purchase in Fairfield, I had already received a job offer in Palo Alto, CA—about 60 miles to the south. As a result of this new job at a distance, we decided not to move into the Fairfield house but had to scramble to figure out what we would do. We settled on keeping our new house and renting it out to a colonel, a pilot who had just returned from Vietnam. Having decided to move south, we rented a house near my new job. After six months of renting, we found and bought a new-construction home in Sunnyvale, California. So, within a year of that first, tentative step of purchasing our first home in Fairfield, we were now owners of two homes.

This serendipitous, initial real estate experience emboldened Mary Ann and me to educate ourselves to continue our journey as "real-estate investors." Yes, it can be scary since the cash outlays and bank commitments (loans) can be quite large, but with proper planning, you can mitigate the risk of these transactions. Having been a "planner" for so long, my mind was trained to evaluate these situations logically and methodically. Once you break down real-estate investments to their most basic components, it becomes much easier to visualize and manage the risk and the reward.

If you think about it, every life decision is a "risk-reward" decision. Even though you're not consciously aware of it, even a trip to the corner store for a gallon of milk has a risk and a reward. If the road to the store is perilous and icy, you might unconsciously calculate that the trip to get milk is too great a risk—and you don't go. The milk can wait for another day! However, if your baby needed the milk and it was essential enough to get some, you might decide that in light of the circumstances, you're willing to take that risk—and you go.

Whether just living life or attempting to undertake serious investment choices, we need to become adept at making these risk-reward calculations. Like everything in life, we get better at is as we educate ourselves, apply this knowledge to opportunities. But above all, we must continuously practice, practice, practice. The ability to adopt and practice this skill will yield results that observers will see as "lucky!" However, we know that it is the result of hard work, study and perseverance.

Our next real estate move, two years later, was to sell the Fairfield house. It had appreciated quite a bit, and Mary Ann and I thought that it would be smart to cash out and buy two homes in Suisun, CA., next door to Fairfield, where homes were a little less expensive. In hindsight, had we known we were going to stay in Sunnyvale, I would have bought those two homes here, for only a little bit more money. At the time, we thought we might be returning to the Fairfield area, and this is why we purchased there. Sunnyvale properties have appreciated much more than those in Fairfield. The lesson here is location, location, location.

By this time, I was settled into my new job, and I was getting regular pay raises at six-month intervals. Mary Ann and I had figured out that real-estate investing was a good way forward. Our thought was to move cautiously, in stages, and methodically purchasing one rental at a time as funds became available. We felt that, through this plan, we could make extra money for retirement, resulting in enough funds to live well the remainder of our lives and to provide for our family for generations to come.

Again, the ability to focus and carefully consider possible ramifications of decisions as well as the ability to implement mitigation strategies to reduce the risk is paramount to success. I cannot overemphasize the role that education, mentorship (if available) and prayerful consideration play in this endeavor. The need for education should be self-evident by now. Seeking "mentorship" and "prayerful consideration" both speak to your level maturity and wisdom.

To me, "maturity and wisdom" lead to confident decision-making. This does not mean that, in our decisions, there won't be mistakes or need for path corrections, but it does mean that we will be confident in our decisions as we have a plan. Our willingness to be humble and seek guidance from mentors or from our creator speaks volumes about our state of mind as we move forward. Do we think we have all the answers, or do we concede that we fall short and could use some help? This is the difference between being "confident" and being "arrogant". Confident is good; arrogant is bad.

In the late 1970's and early 1980's, my wife and I bought another rental in Sunnyvale and then started buying rental property in the Sunshine state of Texas—two houses in Houston and one in San Antonio. This area was marketed heavily in California as the next up-and-coming "hot investment." This venture, however, did not do so well. Because of the distance, I could not control my expenses and had little ability to vet tenants. We decided to sell the Texas rentals and purchase property near our home for ease of management. During this period, my wife inherited her parents' home in Bryan, Texas. After the lessons we had learned about "distance management", we soon sold that property also.

Upon selling the Texas properties, we used the money to buy two houses in California—one in Fremont and another in Milpitas. Because of earthquakes, we diversified the property locations to mitigate the effects of "a big one" striking a particular area. We also sold the Sunnyvale rental around this time as it was not an area of economic growth. We used the equity to purchase a third rental in San Jose. I still own these three properties, and they have done very well for me.

In 2017, I sold both the Suisun properties and conducted a 1031 exchange in order to buy a new, 4-bedroom condominium in Milpitas. Now, all of my rentals are within easy driving distance of my home, easy for me to manage, but still far enough apart in distance that I feel they are diversified by location.

I have done well with real estate over the years. Currently, I feel, the real-estate market has become overpriced and I hesitate to continue adding to those investments. It is important to continuously assess your strategy and to be willing, and nimble enough, to make the necessary changes. At 96, I continue to read real state material in newspapers, keep abreast of the local home prices and constantly look for excellent home buys. As the saying goes, "if you are not studying, contemplating and looking for new avenues, you are dying."

Real estate represents a large portion of my investment portfolio. I believe that it provides security because the value of the investment principal is tied to inflation. As inflation rises, so do property values and rents. But, real estate is only one of the eggs in the basket. I also invest in the "market" as I believe in diversification. Not only is it a common-sense principle, but it is also taught in the Bible.

"Divide your portion to seven, or even eight, for you do not know what misfortune may occur on the earth"

Solomon speaking, Ecclesiastes 11:2

Following the concept of diversification is wise. The Bible teaches us that the *"fear of the Lord is the beginning of wisdom" Proverbs 9:10*. To me, the word "fear" as it is used in this passage means respect or consideration. I have held throughout my life that prayer is essential to fulfilling God's plan for me, specifically, and for his people, generally. Deviating from God's plan is foolish and demonstrates a certain amount of arrogance. Many people would argue with my analysis, but I'm convinced that we will all find out, in the end, who "read it right." Additionally, I believe that my personal experience points to the veracity of my belief.

My "portion" is divided among real-estate holdings in different markets and locations. I also have a "portion" invested in stocks and bonds as well as a cash reserve to take advantage of investment opportunities. Additionally, I have two pensions—three if you count Social Security. All of this did not occur because of "luck", it occurred because of a lot of hard work and planning. It is somewhat subjective how I define or count the number of "portions" that I own. But, by my count, I have about eight…. I'm in the ball-park! I tell you this not to "brag", but to encourage you to be wise. *"Blessed are those who find wisdom, those who gain understanding"* **Proverbs 3:13**

The concept of diversification is universally accepted as a wise method of spreading out risk. We've heard the saying "don't put all of your eggs in one basket," the reason being is that, if we drop the basket, all of the eggs will break, resulting in a poor outcome. If you distribute your eggs in several baskets and subsequently drop one of the baskets, the remaining eggs will still be intact and you will have only lost a small portion of the whole. Not only is this principle taught in the Bible, but wise professors also teach this in business school.

The early formal education that I received complemented the lessons that my family taught me as a child. The experience I gained from my military training further re-enforced those views. My later college business classes and eventually my post-graduate business-administration training fully cemented and solidified my belief in saving, investing and diversification. But I also learned so much more.

CHAPTER 8

A New Chapter

My MBA education had prepared me to be a financial analyst at Philco Ford, for which I was grateful. Philco Ford filled many government contracts, and I was to gather and organize financial data for the four contracts I had been assigned. This data would help me to analyze our business performance (were we efficient, effective and profitable?), to project cost expenditures for the immediate future in order to help management anticipate profitability (or loss) and to alert management when they exceed their budget.

While my Golden Gate University degree had prepared me well, there is always a gap between theory and practice. Always a learning period in adapting to a specific, new work situation. Being who I was, and not given to exerting a half-effort, I invested a lot of energy into launching into this new job because I was intent on coming up to speed quickly in my new career. I was used to being an "A-player!" By early 1975, after a few months at Philco Ford working as a financial analysis, the interactions and requirements of my new job became second nature to me. Both my previous work habits and my MBA combined to allow me to adjust well to my new surroundings.

While Brenda was away to College, she met and married Bill Crosthwaite. Brenda finished college, completed a business course and worked as a mortgage manager for a local company. Bill worked as a Loan Collector. They had one child, Sara, and continued to live in the Garland, TX area throughout their lives. Early in my new career, I traveled and worked for a short period in TX and was able to visit regularly as Sara was growing up. Mary Ann did not travel with me for work, but she would fly out with me a couple of times a year while I was on vacation.

In 1976, Philco Ford changed its name to Ford Aerospace and Communication (Ford Aerospace) as the company tried to get into the developing High-Tech sector. Later in the decade, I was assigned additional responsibilities (without extra pay) as contract administrator, all while still working as a financial analyst. As contract administrator, I now prepared both sales and purchase contracts. This involved negotiating contractual terms with new business and updating contracts with new existing partners. The two jobs seemed to work well side by side. I have fond memories handling million-dollar contracts and depositing million-dollar checks in the bank for Ford Aerospace. At the time, my managers hoped to move me entirely into contracts, but this never happened.

In 1979, however, I was moved into another job requiring weather experience. On September 22, 1979, there had been a suspected, major atomic explosion off the coast of South Africa. At that point, the US became interested in developing Nuclear Test sensors to be placed on US satellites. They contracted with Ford Aerospace, who already had an existing Satellite contract with the US government, to develop detection capability for nuclear test activity around the Globe. Until these new sensors were developed, the project called for a weather expert to join the ranks of the many other professionals who would be working on this report. Weather anomalies was how nuclear blasts were detected prior to the development of dedicated nuclear sensors.

Before I could start working with the meteorology crew, the Human Resources department at Ford Aerospace, being the large bureaucratic corporation it was, had to re-classify me as a scientist since the weather job was in a different department than finance. The re-classification was not a stretch because of my previous work-experience in the Air Force; I felt right at home in my new tasks. This first weather project, after a few years of being away from the field, required a rapid and intense study period. My new boss, John Blake, called me from Florida during a meeting he was attending and asked me to prepare a study as quickly as I could to verify that an atomic explosion had occurred off the coast of South Africa[6]. Mr. Blake said that it

---

6   From Wikipedia ...[A]n unidentified double flash of light [was] detected by an American Vela Hotel satellite on 22 September 1979 near the Prince Edward Islands in the Indian Ocean. The cause of the flash remains officially unknown, and some information about the event remains classified. While it has been suggested that the signal could have been caused by a meteoroid hitting the satellite, the previous 41 double flashes detected by the Vela satellites were caused by nuclear weapons tests. Today, most independent researchers believe that the 1979 flash was caused by a nuclear explosion— perhaps an undeclared nuclear test carried out by South Africa and Israel.

was important to obtain and study all the surface and upper air data as soon as possible to ascertain the location of this detonation. If I could verify that this information contained evidence of atomic materials, Mr. Blake wanted me to present my findings in person to the House of Representatives Sub Committee on Intelligence. Because of the urgency, I immediately started to assemble all the atmosphere data available from the National Weather Service, Pacific Command Forecast Center, satellite reports, the European-Weather Service, to include surface, upper air, satellite and thermal data. Although the US Air Force had sent an aircraft to collect upper air samples, their findings had been taken eighteen hours after the explosion. By that time, all or most all of the remains had integrated into the atmosphere, providing little evidence of a nuclear detonation.

I worked diligently on this project for six months looking for any idea or data that would help prove an atomic explosion had occurred. I could not find any evidence on the surface or the atmosphere to prove this. Later, I learned how the country that had detonated the explosion. They cleverly detonated their device soon after the scheduled surface and upper air observations were taken by satellites. This timing allowed them to conceal their identity. Normally, metrological observations are taken every 12 hours, and this explosion happened after the American South to North satellites passed the area. As a result, no observations were taken immediately after the explosion. By the time they were taken, eleven hours had gone by, leaving much time for the debris, heat and shock waves to be integrated into the atmosphere, thus erasing the evidence.

While I gained a lot of experience working on this South Africa project, I was disappointed not to be able to arrive at a specific conclusion. It would have been an honor to present my findings to a subcommittee of the US House, if concrete evidence had been available.

After the investigation was terminated in 1980, I concluded South Africa was most likely the country that detonated the atomic bomb but I could not prove this conclusively. My observations pointed in that direction, however. South Africa was in proximity to the point of the explosion, they could have moved their equipment very easily under night cover. Since they knew our weather observation satellites schedules, they could conduct their tests when no satellites were overhead. They knew that this would make it nearly impossible for the US to prove that South Africa had conducted a nuclear detonation test. They also needed to test their latest weapons development to gain superiority over neighboring countries. For all of these reasons, South Africa was the logical culprit.

I have been curious all these years wondering if my original thoughts and conclusions were correct that South Africa was to blame. I got an answer while on a trip to South Africa in November 2016. The program director of my travel group confirmed that South Africa did explode an atomic bomb in the period I had studied but he said the country had ceased its development and testing immediately because of adverse world opinion.

While work consumed a lot of my day, I had tasks during my off time too. I was a Deacon for our congregation and took care of the church's financial records for a number of years. Mary Ann was also active in Christian ministry and had many friends who called her daily. Several times a month, we would have parish meetings at our home.

Jerry was somewhat interested in softball and I would accompany him to his practices and games. I also spent a lot of time making car and home repairs. Additionally, I bought and managed several rental properties as I attempted to secure our financial future. I was accustomed to long hours of work in order to provide for my family. My father had ingrained this ethic into my young mind. As I reflect on my work-life choices and if I had to redo it all, I would not change a thing.

Sometime after the South Africa study, around 1984, I joined a team of 8 engineers and scientists to help prepare a proposal to build a weather satellite for India. The Indian government was interested in acquiring a Synchronous Meteorological Satellite (SMS), developed by Ford Aerospace, that had been launched from Cape Canaveral, Florida, for the U.S. Military, NASA and independent contractors. This satellite was designed to detect meteorological data from a fixed altitude of 22,000 miles above the surface and to continuously monitor broad areas of the earth, obtain day and night data and help predict local weather events: including thunderstorms, fog, hurricanes/typhoons, flash floods and other severe weather conditions. The Indian government wanted to buy a similar satellite to serve their commercial and military uses.

We worked for several months on a proposal to present to the Indian Government before flying to India for the presentation. At this point in my life, with all of the military travel I had done, I did not give the novelty of this trip much thought. I had a job to do. For my part, I prepared power point slides to depict the surface and upper level weather maps including other charts that could be used in their commercial and military operation. Actually, I presented a weather briefing and forecast for a particular time showing how it could be used effectively for both commercial and military use. The other engineers and scientists presented briefings relating to their specialty.

Our original proposal to build and launch a weather satellite for the Indian government was for 10 million dollars. During the negotiations, the Indian Government asked for a reduction in cost to 6 million dollars, as this was the total amount authorized for the project. We contacted Ford Aerospace officials in California, and their answer was that we could not go any lower than 10 million dollars.

As a result, another contractor from Southern California won the contract and started working immediately, but after three or four months, that company could not provide the software needed to make the overall system work. The Indian Government then contacted Ford Aerospace to ask if we could resume developing the software and pick up the contract. By then, they were willing to pay the full $10 million. However, it was too late, our team had been disbanded, members were committed to working on other contracts and could not be reassigned. If we had won the contract when we were ready to do the work, the plan had been for the team to stay in India for two years, get the satellite and all the systems associated with it operating smoothly and then negotiate a new contract for additional work. But that, of course, did not happen.

After returning from India where I had been for my part of the presentation on the SMS project, and since we had not won that work, management assigned me to work in logistics. A major shipment of equipment, material and resources was anticipated for another project. I was to ensure rapid and accurate delivery of equipment and to review and record shipping documents. Additionally, we had to identify redundancies and to assure the quality of what was delivered. I made numerous trips to San Pedro, California, to work in logistics there on this ongoing contract.

While at San Pedro, I had the opportunity to witness a movie being filmed across the street from the building where I was working. The main actress was Goldie Hawn. I saw all the outside activities, bright lights, large filming trucks, a lot of personnel movement, but not Goldie Hawn because of their restrictions.

Once the San Pedro job was completed, I was asked to travel to Dallas, Texas, to work on more logistical tasks similar to San Pedro's. This job only lasted 6 months. This was a wonderful opportunity to visit Brenda, Bill and Sara.

Subsequently, I was asked to participate in the early development of an important project called Global Positioning System (GPS). GPS was being developed at that time. The use of a constellation, or multiple, satellites would allow for the triangulation of a position anywhere on Earth. There was a lot of interest in the concept because at the time satellites were transmitting messages worldwide but only through a single satellite which cannot be used to triangulate a position. The Air Force asked Ford Aerospace to organize, manage and record all the activities related to this new technology. Originally, Ford's main interest in this development was to install a sensor aboard a satellite to detect nuclear explosions. Since the Air Force requested Ford get more involved, management accepted the responsibility.

My primary job on this project was to record all discussions and conclusions from each of the meetings and formulate specifications resulting from these meetings. Meetings were scheduled every two weeks and held in Palo Alto, California. There were approximately 18 members from different organizations throughout the United States on this project.

The plan was to launch 18 satellites and to have three spare satellites in orbit that could be moved into position to replace a satellite that was malfunctioning. Since this concept was new, and had never been used before, there were some really hot arguments about the satellite's functionality, operation and reliability. The final decision was to build 18 satellites with three spares and to launch them as planned, but after gaining some operational experience, the U.S. Government increased the number of satellites to 24. This allowed for a 95% operational reliability. To ensure redundancy, the Air Force eventually launched 31 operational GPS satellites. At any given time, every satellite may not be operational.

GPS satellites orbit at an altitude of approximately 12,550 miles. They were to have been positioned at 22,000 miles, but this did not work so they moved the position closer to earth. The satellites in the GPS constellation now are arranged into six equally spaced orbital planes surrounding the Earth. Each plane contains four "slots" occupied by baseline satellites. This ensures users can view at least four satellites from any point on the planet.

When we first worked on developing this concept of GPS satellites into a product, we did not realize that it would affect every aspect of modern life. GPS technology is now in everything from cell phones, wristwatches, bulldozers, shipping containers and ATM's. It is used in the economy, farming, construction, mining, surveying, logistics, banking and wireless technology to name a few. GPS is used in weather forecasting, earthquake monitoring and environmental protection agencies. Finally, GPS is critical to our national security, integrated into every facet of our military operations, from munitions to vehicles. New uses of GPS are invented every day and are limited only by our imaginations. I am grateful that I had a small part in developing the GPS, it is one of my life's greatest achievements to have been a part of this great development.

After this time, the Air Force decided to move all its satellite tracking to Colorado Springs, Colorado, and by doing so, all the management was to be performed at one location, within one system. This transfer was to connect the subsystem in Sunnyvale, California, to the larger system in Colorado Springs, Colorado. I was assigned to participate in this project and so I moved to the Sunnyvale office. Since I arrived in the later part of the move to Colorado, my participation was minimal. My primary function was to track the movement of equipment and to do quality assurance.

By 1986, Mary Ann had developed an ovarian cancer that required surgery. When the surgeon performed the exploratory surgery, he found that the cancer had metastasized throughout most of her body. After the surgery, the surgeon came to me and said that he wanted to talk. We went outside onto the balcony. He told me that her case was very serious and that he was not able to remove the entire cancer. In this conversation, the oncologist told me that my wife only had two years to live. What followed was an emotional roller-coaster ride for us.

The surgeon was correct in his assessment as Mary Ann lived only two years from the time of her surgery. Her death was from a combination of lupus and ovarian cancer with ovarian cancer being the primary cause. Mary Ann passed on 18 July,1988.

I was devastated... My dream of retiring with my loved one was gone. It took me several months to adjust after the close relationship of 32 years. I went to her gravesite, took flowers which I left near her stone, polished her bronze headstone each week for months and reminisced about our life together. After a long adjustment to a life without my dear wife Mary Ann, I came to the realization that life has to move forward and I had better move forward and lead a productive life. Besides my work at Ford Aerospace, I got involved in purchasing more real estate, taking courses at a local college and participating in local activities. These are interests that I have continued to pursue all these years.

A year after Mary Ann passed, I met a wonderful lady by the name of Dr. Rosita K. Serra. We had a wonderful relationship and she helped me overcome my recent loss with her friendship and companionship. I helped her with her real estate and she helped me with mine. Together, we traveled overseas, attended college classes, dancing classes and local events. We continued this close relationship until November 2015 when she moved to Seattle to live in a retirement home, near her daughter Vivianne. Since then, she has transferred into a memory-care facility. I miss her very much but we talk almost weekly via phone. I am still interested in her wellbeing and happiness. I visit her each year.

In 1988, Ford Aerospace was sold to Loral, and shortly after, Lockheed Martin bought Loral, so I became an employee of the new owners. After moving to Lockheed Martin in San Jose, California, I served as a Documentation Specialist with responsibility for maintaining company documents pertaining to the software development that was being worked on for the US government. I had a crew of four employees who helped me to store, catalogue and retrieve all the documents related to this project. In working this project, it was difficult to get a good handle on the software version because there were constant changes taking place—even daily. Of the 100 software engineers working on this project, a third were working the midnight shift. When I finished a test phase at the end of a day, I expected to resume my work the next morning. Often, however, the midnight team made drastic changes on the software. When I resumed my test the next morning, the software did not work as intended until I recognized the changes that had occurred and made the appropriate adjustments.

It took our team a long time to complete this task since we had to wait until all tests were completed and approved before writing the final software version. It appeared that my team and I were taking two steps forward and one step back during the development. After much back and forth, tests were performed and the software was approved and shipped to the US government office in Los Angeles, California… two years had gone by.

Sometime During this period, my son Jerry married Carolyn Thomas on January 27, 1996. They adopted one child, Janelle, and currently live in Tracy, California.

After completing the Software Test task, I realized that I enjoyed that type of work, and I continued working in System Engineering for the next ten years at Lockheed Martin. My main responsibilities in this field were consulting with clients, determining business needs, ensuring system security, collaborating with other departments, testing software and hardware systems plus monitoring their performance.

My job involved a variety of tasks that required a combination of abilities such as analysis, communication, business skills, new system implementation, correcting software errors and conducting hardware upgrades.

Additionally, I would like to identify the following "Certificate of Training Courses", I received while working in the Aerospace Industry:

- Engineering Inspection Refresher Course, dated 17th August 2000
- Engineering Methodology Overview, dated 3rd August 2000
- SE – CMM (System Engineering – Communicate Management Monitoring) overview   Training, dated 31st August 2000
- Peer Review Tool (PRT) Training, dated 24th August 2000

- SW – CMM (Software – Communication Management Monitoring, dated 13th September 2000

- PRICE Hardware Model, Software Model, used to project life cycle cost of hardware components for large proposals and other projects, dated March 1987. I worked in Price for several years projecting life cycle cost of hardware components for proposal pricing.

- DOORS 4.1 Distribution of Operational Resources

- dated 26th – 27th June 2000

- System Engineering Handbook Training, dated 5th December 1997

Throughout my Aerospace career, I was assigned to many different projects because management felt that I had the interest, skills, ability, experience and determination required to perform these tasks. I felt that management appreciated my efforts because they knew that if they assigned me to a particular task, I would see it to completion. I appreciated the opportunity to work for Ford Aerospace, Loral and Lockheed Martin during my last 26 years of work. I retired from Lockheed in January, 2001. I feel satisfied and complete knowing that I did my best while working continuously for 52 years, 26 years in the military plus 26 years in aerospace. I am very grateful for the many opportunities and adventures I had, starting in the Air Force and ending with Lockheed Martin.

CHAPTER 9

Travel Experiences

One of the benefits of my financial planning and investment strategy is the extra cash flow that has allowed me to indulge my interest in travel. I don't travel just for the sake of traveling; I plan and research my getaways with an eye towards furthering my education and increasing my understanding of the world. I have circled the globe once, and have visited 52 of the 195 countries of the world. At the pace of one-country-a-year, I will have visited them all by the time I turn 234.

Here is a list of all my non-military travel:

- The Blue Danube, Budapest to Prague.
- Alpine Europe and villages.
- Eastern Europe and the Black Sea.
- Cruise of the Rhine and Mosel Rivers.
- Argentina to Chile
- Russia: Volga River cruise.
- China and the Yangtze River.
- Chile, Argentina and Uruguay
- Russia and Baltic: St Petersburg, Moscow, Estonia
- Nordic coastal cruise: Sweden, Norway, Finland, Arctic Circle. (When crossing into the Arctic Circle, it is customary to give a toast with a strange concoction of fish-oil and alcohol. It is supposed to be good luck. The back cover of my memoir has a picture of me extending a toast to your health.)
- South Africa: Cape Town, (then I had my accident)
- Aegean and Mediterranean Seas: Athens to Jerusalem and Greek islands.
- Transatlantic Cruise (with Brenda)

On my 2016 trip to South Africa, I accidentally fell as I stepped off the safari truck and broke my leg. That "misstep" resulted in a visit to a local hospital, a surgery to screw in a metal rod to hold my femur together and a first-class flight back home to the USA with a nurse attendant by my side. Once back, I spent time in a convalescent home followed by months of physical therapy to get me back up-and-running. Quite an exciting "trip" that year. Through 2017, I fully healed from that fall but I did not travel. In 2018, I "got back on the horse" and I traveled to Greece and Israel.

During November 2018, I completed a voyage that included the countries of Greece, Cyprus and Israel plus several islands in the Eastern Mediterranean and Aegean Seas.

While in Greece, I had the opportunity to visit Corinth (where Apostle Paul was tried), Patmos, and the cave where Apostle John lived and wrote the Book of Revelation, Nauplion (the old capital of Greece in ancient times), and Mycenae (King Agamemnon ruled over this city which was built 3500 years ago). We visited the statue of Asclepius, the God of Medicine. We drove to Olympia and stood in the first Olympic stadium, the birthplace of the Olympic games. We visited an olive oil factory and observed how olive oil is extracted. We had a guided tour of the Acropolis of Athens with the Parthenon and the Erechtheion. We walked the same foot-steps as Plato, Aristotle, Socrates, Alexander III and many other famous people who lived or visited there centuries ago. This area, as described above, is known or referred to as the cradle of the Western Civilization.

During the Mediterranean and Aegean Seas voyage, we stopped at the islands of Santorini with its white-washed, cube-formed houses, and blue-domed chapels. The island of Symi with pink, blue and yellow houses, beautiful beaches and fantastic music festivals. And Rhodes, once home of the Colossus of Rhodes which was considered one of the seven wonders of the world. It is the largest Greek Island, known for its beautiful beaches and ancient ruins. Lastly, Cyprus. I admired the luxurious homes still intact in the city of Paphos. We tasted many delightful Greek pastries, and the food was fantastic.

After the Greek Islands, we cruised to Haifa, Israel. While in Israel, we visited Mount of Olive, the City of David, the Dead Sea, observed the Dead

Sea Scrolls, visited the tomb of Jesus and the Western Wall, known as the "Wailing Wall of the Jews." This was a wonderful and memorable trip. I hope that the memories I acquired and the new friends I made will last for decades.

In 2019 I traveled from Prague, through to Germany, boarded a cruise ship to the Baltics, to Denmark, Scotland, Iceland, Nova Scotia and ending in New York City. I guess the biggest surprises on my last trip were the size of the vessel (1043.32 ft), the total mileage traveled (nearly 7,000 miles) and the number of people aboard (nearly 7,000 passengers). It was a memorable trip. To keep abreast of all the activities, I walked between one and two miles onboard each day. This cruise was special since my daughter, Brenda, accompanied me.

One of the best parts of traveling is that the journey never really ends. I'm always looking for my next great adventure and look forward to exploring new horizons. By traveling, I gain a better understanding of different civilizations. This helps me interact and connect with folks back home. They say America is a melting pot of cultures, and I have found this to be true.

Many times, while looking for someone to complete a project in one of my rentals, I've had to interact with immigrants to this country. When this happens, I find that my travel experiences help with the transaction. I can empathize and communicate much better as a result. I am able to fully engage in each conversation and focus my attention on the here-and-now. Sometimes a smile, a laugh, or a grimace is all it takes to get through to someone. One is forced to hone those skills when traveling abroad in a land where one does not speak the language.

Traveling is good for one's soul. Scientific studies provide evidence that a vacation is great for mental and physical health, relieves stress and helps one cope with everyday problems. As for me, travel gives me perspective and an appreciation for what I have at home; it opens my eyes to new possibilities and ways of thinking. All of this gives me peace and joy. It may be hard for some of you to believe but even at my current age of 96, the adventure aspect of travel still excites me. While reading, I've come across some great travel quotes with which I very much agree. Here are a few:

"Twenty years from now, you will be more disappointed by the things that you didn't do than by the ones you did do. So, throw off the bowlines. Sail away from the safe harbor. Catch the trade winds in your sails. Explore. Dream. Discover."

— Mark Twain

"Only those who risk going too far can possibly find out how far they can go."

— T.S. Eliot

"Life's journey is not to arrive at the grave safely in a well-preserved body. But rather to skid in sideways, totally worn out, shouting, "What a ride!"

— Anonymous

The Acknowledged continents of the globe are: Europe, Africa, North America, Antarctica, Asia, South America, Oceania and Australia. Of these, I still need to visit Antarctica, Oceania and Australia. I will plan to visit these soon.

I have enjoyed traveling to all of the destinations I've visited. My most memorable experiences have been my travel through Central Europe Switzerland, Austria and France. I thought that Switzerland was really beautiful in the summer, flowers growing in pots outside windows and balconies, breathtaking mountain lakes and very friendly people. My visit through Austria and France brought back thoughts of WWII and all of the associated problems. To look at those vibrant countries now is nothing short of miraculous! A testament to the human spirit. I traveled through Eastern Europe and Russia twice, both times on river cruises. Yugoslavia was also memorable in that Rosita and I were among the first "Westerners" to travel on Josip Broz Tito's, now refurbished private train. It was quite plush as it had opulent staterooms, bathrooms and dining cars. Quite the experience.

I also enjoyed the culture and sights of South America, especially

Peru and Chile. The people were friendly and personable. Peru's Machu Picchu was awe-inspiring. To think that an early culture could build such a complex citadel at the top of the world! The Chilean people made wonderful empanadas, a bun-like pastry with either chicken or beef inside: great eating!

As I travel, I sometimes reflect on what makes civilizations and cultures similar, and what makes them different. Through my meteorologist's prism, I've observed that the variations in climate in different regions and locations can have an impact on societal norms. It seems to me that colder climates foster more "community" as people congregate for warmth and companionship. In warmer climates, people can operate more on their own, thus allowing for greater personal autonomy and leisure. Warmer climates seem to foster less "community". This increased, individual, leisure time has allowed certain civilizations to engage in greater philosophical pursuits, and a deeper search for knowledge such was the case in Greece, the birthplace of Western Civilization.

My view is that I know man was created in the image and likeness of God. As such, we are most "like God", when we are creating. "Creating" something, or "creating" (synthesizing) new thoughts or concepts. As we venture through life, it therefore seems logical and right that we should consider the direction we should take. Prov 16:9 "A man's heart plans his course, but the Lord directs his steps.". As we manage our lives, who better to consult than the one we will answer to: Our Creator. GOD. More on this in the next chapter.

CHAPTER 10

Leadership

During my 26 years in the military, I was appointed as a leader on many projects. I was chosen because of my rank and my ability to get along with people.

In 1957 when I was only 27, I was placed in charge of 60 men who lived in the same barracks. These barracks were buildings constructed before WWII to house approximately 60 airmen or soldiers sleeping in bunks. As a general rule, each Friday evening a GI "party" is scheduled to clean the barracks thoroughly for an inspection the next day, Saturday.

On the previous Tuesday, I had posted a notice on the bulletin board that a GI "party" was scheduled for 7:00 P.M. Friday night. About a third of the barrack's occupants attended. Because of the poor attendance, I knew the absent men had disobeyed an order. I thought, "If they want to play this game and to test my authority, I will teach these young recruits a lesson."

Discipline is difficult to enforce, especially in large groups of teen and young 20-year-olds, most having their first experience away from home. Leadership requires an ability to use circumstances to teach a lesson. Most of the time, the natural consequences of an action are the best way to teach a lesson. Leaders need to draw connections between behaviors (action) and consequences. That night, I saw my opportunity to exercise leadership with this unit. A unit is a "team" which succeeds or fails together. This is an important, general concept in the military—one that is not generally practiced by civilians, other than in team sports.

Lights were out at 10:00 P.M. but at 12:00 P.M. that night, I turned on all the lights, ordered all out of bed and to fall into formation outside in 10 minutes. The weather wasn't nice, as it had been raining all day. I marched them to the parade ground in mud and rain. We marched in formation until 2:00 A.M. Then, after that, the men cleaned the barracks to be ready for the open rank inspection, as well as the barracks inspection, which was scheduled for 8:00 A.M. The inspection was conducted by the commanding officer of all of the "flights". (A "flight' is the basic unit in the Air Force. Several "flights" comprise a "squadron". The Squadron Commander is the Commanding Officer.) No one missed a GI party from that time forward.

Another instance occurred in 1972 when I was chief weather forecaster at Travis Air Force Base in California. I was in charge of one major, two captains, one lieutenant and several sergeants. It was a very demanding job in which I briefed the commanding general and his staff each morning at 7:00 A.M., prepared a 24-hour work schedule, briefed pilots during the day plus attended to personnel matters among employees. This was during the Vietnam War period. I also had two retired Lieutenant Colonels working under me too. Since I was a Chief Master Sargent and the officers outranked me, they didn't object because it was less work for them. We all got along very well and the workload was heavy as we had 1500 weather briefings each month (with most of the flights headed to Vietnam). This amount of work cannot be achieved without the leader training and motivating his men to work this hard.

In 1980, after leaving the military, I was in charge of a documentation group at Ford Aerospace to summarize and document software development for the government. I had about seven people helping me in this endeavor. There were nearly 50 software programmers. We completed the job on time without difficulty.

During my two careers, I have had opportunity both to be a leader and to observe the leadership of others. While I have had a sense of what good leadership is, I have wanted to write about it both to define my own thinking and to help others to understand what leadership is.

We need to define leadership. Webster's defines leadership as "the position, function or guidance of a leader." A leader has to have the ability to listen to his people, too. Generally, a "leader" who does not listen to his people and who does not include their concerns and inputs into the solution of problems is not a leader. He is the head of a bunch of minions. Eventually, the organization will become ineffective as individuals show up to work to do the bare minimum to receive a paycheck.

A great believer in the Bible, I turned to it to see what it might offer us about leadership. I found that there are approximately 50 verses referring to leadership in the Bible. I would like to present a few of these verses to expand my view of leadership.

Here are Biblical quotes I found:

1. A leader delegates to other capable leaders.

"Select capable men from all people – men who fear God, trustworthy men who hate dishonest gain and appoint them as officials over thousands, hundreds, fifties and tens."

— Exodus 18.2.

2. A leader's integrity comes from within.

"And David shepherded them with integrity of heart; with skillful hands, he led them."

— Psalm 78:72.

3. Leaders pay special attention to their resources.

"Be sure you know the condition of your flocks, give careful attention to your herds: for riches do not endure forever, and a crown is not secure for all generations."

— Proverbs 27:23–24.

"Resources don't last forever. Money gets spent, volunteers move on, and facilities and systems break down. The church needs leaders who are keeping track of these resources to make sure they're plentiful and healthy!"

— E. Woolum

4. Leaders recognize their limitations.

"For my thoughts are not your thoughts, neither are your ways my ways," declares the Lord. "As the heavens are higher than the earth, so are my ways higher than your ways and my thoughts than your thoughts."

— Isaiah 55:8-9.

"Face it – you are fallible. You don't have all the answers, even if everyone thinks you do. Another reason we need to be investing in our spiritual sensitivity is because as soon as we start trusting in our own wisdom, we're sunk."

— E. Woolum

5. Leadership is about justice, mercy, and humility.

"So, in everything, do to others what you would have them do to you for this sums up the Law and the Prophets."

— Matthew 7:12.

"The golden rule isn't particular to Christianity, but Jesus adds a new wrinkle to it. Instead of it being a prohibition (don't do to others what you don't want them to do to you), Jesus instructs us to do for others what we wish they would do for us."

"This mindset should epitomize all of our leadership. After all, it sums up the whole law."

— E. Woolum

6. A real leader is the servant of all.

"You call me 'Teacher' and 'Lord,' and rightly so, for that is what I am. Now that I, your Lord and Teacher, have washed your feet, you also should wash one another's feet. I have set you an example that you should do as I have done to you. Very truly I tell you, no servant is greater than his master, nor is a messenger greater than the one who sent him. Now that you know these things you will be blessed if you do them."

— John 13:13-17.

7. A leader learns to be content in every situation.

"I know what it is to be in need, and I know what it is to have plenty. I have learned the secret of being content in any and every situation, whether well fed or hungry, whether living in plenty or in want. I can do all this through him who gives me strength."

— Philippians 4:12-13.

"Too often people quote Philippians 4:13 as if it stands alone. But Paul is setting himself up as an example of contentment in leadership. We can't look at our current experience to gauge God's pleasure or the effectiveness of our work. Sometimes we will experience comfort and sometimes we will suffer want. The key is to find our contentment in serving well, and to avoid judging our success by looking at our situation."

— E. Woolum

8. Lead by keeping your eyes on the goal.

"Join with me in suffering, like a good soldier of Christ Jesus. No one serving as a soldier gets entangled in civilian affairs, but rather tries to please his commanding officer."

— 2 Timothy 2:3-4.

9. A leader's life is an example.

"Remember your leaders, who spoke the word of God to you. Consider the outcome of their way of life and imitate their faith."

— Hebrews 13:7.

10. A leader turns to God for wisdom.

"If any of you lacks wisdom, you should ask God, who gives generously to all without finding fault, and it will be given to you."

— James 1:5.

I also looked to literature and politics for explanations of leadership. The following are poems and statements from prominent authors and leaders:

"Come to the edge.

"We can't. We are afraid.

"Come to the edge.

"We can't. We will fall.

"Come to the edge.

"They came,

"And he pushed them,

"And they flew!"

— Guillaume Apollinaire

"A teacher affects eternity; he can never tell where his influence stops."

— Henry Brooks Adams

"An army of a thousand is easy to find, but ah, how difficult to find a general."

— Chinese proverb

"The very essence of leadership is that you have a vision."

— Theodore Hesburgh

"The world will not belong to managers or those who can make the numbers dance. The world will belong to passionate, driven leaders— people who not only have enormous amounts of energy but who also can energize those whom they lead."

— Jack Welch

"Men make history, and not the other way around. In periods where there is no leadership, society stands still. Progress occurs when courageous, skillful leaders seize the opportunity to change things for the better."

— Harry S. Truman

"Kites rise highest against the wind, not with it."

— Winston Churchill

"Leadership is action, not position."

— Donald H. McGannon

"Be willing to make decisions the best thing you can do is the right thing. The next best thing is the wrong thing, and the worst thing you can do is nothing."

— Theodore Roosevelt

"Leaders do not substitute words for action, do not seek the path of comfort, but face the stress and spur of difficulty and challenge. Leaders learn to stand up in the storm, but to have compassion on those who fail."

— Gen. Douglas McArthur

"Nothing so conclusively proves a man's ability to lead others as what he does from day to day to lead himself."

— Thomas J. Watson

"Do not go where the path may lead. Go instead where there is no path and leave a trail."

— Ralph Waldo Emerson

"A leader takes people where they want to go. A great leader takes people where they don't necessarily want to go, but where they ought to be."

— Rosalynn Carter

"The first responsibility of a leader is to define reality. The last is to say thank you. In between, the leader is a servant."

— Max De Père

"A leader is best when people barely know he exists, not so good when people obey him, worse when they despise him. Fail to honor people, they fail to honor you. But of a good leader who talks little, when his work is done, his aim fulfilled, the people will say, "We did this ourselves."

— Lao-tzu

"Leadership is not a right—it is a responsibility."

— John C. Maxwell

"Do not pray for easy times, pray to be stronger. Do not pray for tasks to equal to your powers, pray for powers equal to your task."

— John F. Kennedy

"The world needs more men who do not have a price at which they can be bought, who do not borrow from integrity to pay for expediency, who have their priorities straight and in proper order, whose handshake is an ironclad contract, who are not afraid of taking risks to advance what is right, and who are as honest in small matters as they are in large ones.

"The world needs more men whose ambitions are big enough to include others, who know how to win with grace and lose with dignity, who do not believe that shrewdness and cunning and ruthlessness are the three keys to success, who still have friends they made twenty years ago, who put principles and consistency above politics or personal advancement, and who are not afraid to go against the grain of popular opinion.

"The world needs more men who do not forsake what is right just to get consensus because it makes them look good, who know how important it is to lead by example, not by barking orders, who would not have you to do something they would not do themselves, who work to turn even the most adverse circumstances into opportunities to learn and improve and who love even those who have done some injustice or unfairness to them. The world, in other words, needs more true leaders."

— Anonymous

"You teach best what you need most to learn."

— Anonymous

CHAPTER 11

Moral Courage

At the end of the day and as life is draws to a close, all you have is you, your integrity and God by your side. In a world where truth seems to be less valued by humans as it once was, there are few people who will tell you the hard truth. When you do meet people with integrity, it is inspirational and reassuring.

You will always be rewarded for courage and integrity; maybe not in this world but you will be rewarded by our creator, God.

Please enjoy the following sayings and poems by the known authors:

"Each time a man stands for an ideal, or acts to improve the lot of others, or strikes out against injustice, he sends forth a tiny ripple of hope, and crossing each other from a million different centers of energy and daring, those ripples build a current that can sweep down the mightiest walls of oppression and resistance."

"Few men are willing to brave the disapproval of their fellows, the censure of their colleagues, the wrath of their society. Moral courage is a rarer commodity than bravery in battle or great intelligence. Yet it is one essential, vital quality for those who seek to change the world that yields most painfully to change."

Robert F. Kennedy

"Are you in earnest? Seize this very minute; Whatever you can do, or dream you can, begin it now; Boldness has genius, power and magic in it."

Johann Wolfgang van Goethe

"Some people see things as they are and say, "Why?"
I dream things that never were and say, "Why not?"

George Bernard Shaw

"No one should negotiate their dreams. Dreams must be free to fly high."

Jesse Jackson

"Go confidently in the direction of your dreams! Live the life you've imagined. As you simply live your life, the laws of the universe will be simpler, solitude will not be solitude, poverty will not be poverty, nor weakness."

Henry David Thoreau

"We cannot become what we need to be by remaining what we are."

Max De Père

"You must be the change you want to see in the world."

Mohandas Gandhi

"If an organization is to meet the challenges of a changing world, it must be prepared to change everything about itself in basic beliefs. ... The only sacred cow in an organization should be its basic philosophy of doing business."

"Thomas J. Watson

"If you want truly to understand something, try to change it."

Kurt Lewin

"If you don't like something, change it. If you can't change it, change your attitude."

Maya Angelou

"The ultimate measure of a man is not where he stands in moments of comfort and convenience, but where he stands in times of challenge and controversy."

Martin Luther King, Jr.

"No one can make you feel inferior without your consent."

Eleanor Roosevelt

"But I know, somehow, that only when it is dark enough, can you see the stars."

Martin Luther King, Jr.

"Some trees grow very tall and straight and large in the forest close to each other, but some must stand by themselves or don't grow at all."

Oliver Wendell Holmes

"Men of integrity try their very existence; rekindle the belief that as a people we can live above the level of moral squalor. We need that belief; a cynical community is a corrupt community."

John W. Gardner

"Courage is being scared to death and saddling up anyway."

John Wayne

"It doesn't interest me what you do for a living. I want to know what you ache for, and if you dare to dream of meeting your heart's longing.

It doesn't interest me how old you are. I want to know if you will risk looking like a fool for love, for your dreams, for the adventure of being alive.

It doesn't interest me who you are, or how you came to be here. I want to know if you will stand in the center of the fire with me and not shrink back."

Oriah Mountain Dreamer

"Always do the things you fear the most. Courage is an acquired taste, like caviar."

Erica Jong

"If you are out to describe the truth, leave elegance to the tailor."

Albert Einstein

"Disobedience is the true foundation of Liberty."

Henry David Thoreau

CHAPTER 12

Success Rules, Laws And Principles

I have used the following success rules, laws and principles for 25 to 30 years to inspire and to guide myself towards my goals. These success rules have helped me to tackle daily challenges, to live with passion and purpose, and to focus on my ambitions.

Success is something everyone wants, and many people spend a lifetime wandering around looking for it with little focus. As a result, they never find the success they long for.

There are fundamental principles for achieving success. They are the same for all people—whether they are unemployed, sales persons, students, homebuyers, high-earning employees or presidents of large companies. They will yield results if diligently applied.

Most of us know the goals we want out of life: a secure retirement, a long life, a successful marriage, excellent health and a loving family. Wanting a goal, however, is not the same as achieving a goal. Only a handful of us have learned to distinguish between the two and how to achieve what we want.

Even at my age, I continue to struggle each day to follow the roadmap of success which I am about to outline for you. I hope that, by your living these principles I am about to enumerate, you will be inspired to look for the pot of gold at the end of the rainbow.

This pot has a name, it is called success.

1. COGITATE, DELIBERATE AND CONTEMPLATE.

A. Always be positive in your daily thinking. Think success and not failure. Beware of negative environments that will lead to trouble and negative people who will pull you down.

Many individuals, companies and organizations fall back on the old adage "It's how we've always done it." Today, we have learned that lessons of the past may not work all that well and companies that don't pay attention to what actually works in the present go by the wayside. This is true in this digital age as it was true in earlier years when I was young. It is easy to fall into a comfortable routine which does not take into account the needs of the present. Without being attuned to the present needs, a person will almost predictably fail at some future point.

B. Always think outside of the box. Don't limit yourself to the way it was always done. Brainstorm possibilities—even outlandish ones. You never know what will stimulate you to a better choice.

Success quotes to be inspired by

"It's what you learn after you 'know it all' that counts. We need to learn to unlearn the things that no longer apply."

— John Wooden, basketball coach, UCLA

"The purpose of life is not to be happy. It is to be useful, to be honorable, to be compassionate, to have it make some difference that you have lived, and lived well."

— Ralph Waldo Emerson, writer

2. DECIDE YOUR TRUE VISION, AMBITION AND PURPOSE IN LIFE TO ESTABLISH BETTER GOALS.

Write down your specific goals and develop a plan to reach them as early as possible in life. Start with the dream you held as a child, teenager or young adult and turn this dream into a series of concrete and carefully crafted goals.

To advance from a dream or an idea to a viable goal, you need a business plan—a roadmap—to provide direction. Many times, in your life, you will wander from the original direction, but it is always best to shift gears and follow your original plan.

When you are eager to attain your vision, it's tempting to plunge in without a rigorous plan. The plan is a framework to all your activities and basis to measure your progress. Taking a seat-of-your-pants approach adds to the risk.

It is not necessary to write a lengthy data-laden document because you may never follow it to a tee. With a busy life, it is difficult to follow written instructions. It is best to write a lean one-page plan for brevity's and clarity's sake. By doing so, you will have the plan with you to review and revise as necessary. The goal is to update your plan annually.

Master the ability to concentrate on what matters most to you and your family, and you're more likely to come away a winner. Once you set a goal, maintain a steady focus on achieving it. When I graduated from high school, I had plans to get into medical school. This did not materialize. I joined the military and applied for West Point. This didn't happen because I was two days too old according to my Representative. My next plan was to get assigned near a military school so I could enroll. I was transferred to Bryan AFB, Texas, which is near Texas A & M University. I enrolled there to attend college during my off-duty time. I was transferred to another post, however, before I could get enough credits from Texas A & M to graduate. I was advancing at a slow pace but I was advancing. Chasing a lofty goal is exhausting and distractions can derail you along the way. It's better to set incremental goals and concentrate on attaining them, one at a time.

Take errors in stride. I responded to my mistakes with an eagerness to learn and grow. By doing so, I feel I'm a better person.

The easiest form of self-sabotage is to focus on what's going wrong, not what's going right. Don't berate yourself but learn from your mistakes and identify what works best for you. Did I use the correct strategy to achieve my original goals? I must have known what I wanted otherwise I would not have acted that way. Always concentrate on clarity of vision. Beware of setting goals in a vacuum. Instead, ask a trusted person to help you distinguish between a realistic goal or target and a pie-in-sky aspiration. Do I have the drive, determination, temperament to accomplish this goal?

While important as explained above, goals themselves have limited value. The real drive of success is how you climb the ladder to attain your objective. Goal setting is not about digging in your heels to reach your objective, but more about the tactics and action steps you take to get there. You must be humble, tactful and personable to succeed. Having a microscope in one eye and a telescope on the other eye would help, too!

Success quote to be inspired by:

"The person who gets it, the person who is going to win, is the person who wants it more."

— Julie Deane, entrepreneur

3.   CONCENTRATE UPON THE COURSE OF ACTION TO TAKE.

Goals that are only written on paper are useless unless actions are taken. Move forward on a plan and don't be afraid to get started. As the old saying states, "Just do it."

You may not succeed the first or second attempt but don't let this stop you. It is known that Ivy League graduates in business have at least one major career setback, yet about 78% of them were able to succeed. They keep plugging along. This may be attributed to excellent judgment, such as discriminating the circumstances and engaging people for impact and/or adapting to the current state of affairs. Developing these skills takes time and effort. The fastest and most effective way to develop any skill is to seek guidance from a coach or mentor.

As I said previously, engage for impact to keep your boss and employees informed, seek accountability, help your associates, develop consistency and continually perfect your abilities.

Even though you have gotten the right job, you may need more than one source of income; but you don't necessarily need more than one job. You may consider other aspects to earn additional income, real estate investment or passive income without spending a lot of money and time.

The following tips are examples to create additional income:

- Spot potential side jobs that do not require a lot of time but provide an additional source of income.

- Parlay your talents into income-producing work.

- Once you have found a new source of income, tweak your current job when necessary and welcome a bird that falls in your hand. Any extra income you can acquire along the way will assist you in retirement.

- Determine your talents and instincts on this new side job. Do you feel comfortable? If not, seek another side job for additional income.

Success quote to be inspired by:

"Pursue one great decision. Aim with force and determination."

— Carl Von Clausewitz, nineteenth-century general

4.   NEVER STOP ACQUIRING KNOWLEDGE.

It is never too late to enroll in school regardless of your age. You should read books, magazines, newspapers or anything to enhance your knowledge. Enroll in formal training classes and acquire skills.

I continue to take courses through the "Great Courses Company," headquartered in Chantilly, Virginia. These courses are taught by outstanding college professors recorded on CD's/DVD's and later reviewed/ studied either while driving or during my spare time at home via TV. Some of the courses I have taken are:

- Understanding Complexity.

- The Art of Critical Decision Making.

- The Life – Death of Stars.

- Roots of Human Behavior.

- Lost World of South America.

- Origins of Great Ancient Civilization.

- Understanding Non-Verbal Communication.

- General Robert E. Lee and his High Command.

- Questions of Value.

- How to Engage and Write About Anything.

- Moral Decision Making.

- The Art of Reading.

The above is a small sample of the large CD/DVD library that I have at home.

5. FOSTER A GOOD RELATIONSHIP WITH YOUR BOSS.

A recent Gallop Poll revealed two reasons people leave their jobs:

- Their manager doesn't help them to succeed.

- Their manager doesn't value them as a human.

If quitting isn't an option, learn to improve your work relationship with the manager and/or other employees. A good relationship with your supervisor is like a puzzle: you have to decide,

- What is important to the boss.

- How you can improve his/her image. Here are some ideas on how to learn to succeed with any type of boss:

A. The Image-Conscious Boss.

Handle this boss with care. You have to be thoughtful and watch your P's and Q's when making contact. If you want your boss to accept you, focus on how your ideas and actions will improve his/her image and present them in that light because your boss really cares about image. This type of boss tends to be successful. They want to impress their own boss in board meetings or during contact with upper level management. If you can function in this environment, you can both learn a lot and move ahead.

B. The Impulsive Boss

Wait for the storm to pass and don't react to every idea he presents. Recognize the good intention he has to offer and respond when you have a good answer and have a good approach. Don't be a "yes" person because he may change his mind very quickly. Don't jump down the rabbit hole either. Wait three or four days before you react to his idea. Pay attention to your boss's rhythm without being a wet blanket.

C. The Pushover Boss

It is very frustrating to learn that your boss won't stand for anything, especially if it is controversial. Step up and offer concrete solutions. Do so in a way that does not threaten your boss.

D. The Incompetent Boss

First, assess if your boss is incompetent. If this proves true, continue to do a good job and don't gossip about your boss's failure. Your words may come back to bite you.

6. KEEP YOUR SKILL SET CURRENT.

The previous five topics in this discussion involved how to get along in the work environment. I'm shifting emphasis and focusing on the future.

According to the Bureau of Labor Statistics, personal health care workers, system engineers, nurses and operational managers are among the jobs with the most growth possibilities.

If you are considering a career change, the best approach is to plan accordingly. The shelf life of any skill is getting shorter and this is due to rapid technological changes. Scientific and technological advances are moving extremely fast. Artificial Intelligence is rather new but this area is expected to expand rapidly and will influence our daily lives tremendously.

I always emphasize—as I do here—to never stop learning. I'm always listening to college courses while driving. I read a lot and subscribe to a lot of educational magazines; Kiplinger, Forbes, Money, Fast, Inc, This Old House, Southern Living, Investor's Business Daily, to name a few. You should too, especially if you are working (and marketing your skills), you should continue to read and expand your knowledge daily.

People who have more information have a tremendous advantage over people who don't. You may think it takes years to acquire the knowledge you would need to become super successful, but the truth is, if you read an hour a day, attend classes and training programs regularly, you can substantially increase your level of knowledge which is directly related to eventual success.

Quotes to be inspired by:

"If I am through learning, I am through."

— John Wooden, basketball coach, UCLA, 10 NCAA championships

"If you want to be happy, tie happiness to a goal, not to people or things."

— Albert Einstein, physicist

7.   MAINTAIN GRIT

The first experience that I can remember to challenge my grit and perseverance was during the spring of 1947 after I graduated from high school. A great flood had destroyed our family home. I wrote about this experience in Chapter 3 of this Memoir. The devastation and the loss of property was so great that many people might have given-up. Instead, three contractors and I began the work of rebuilding. I worked so hard and my clothes were so wet, so sweaty and so dirty that they would almost stand alone when I pulled them off at night. Grit is the force that keeps you going when everything else is telling you to stop.

After this experience, I realized that it was up to me to work, just as hard, to determine my future. Following the Depression, no jobs were available to high school graduates; I decided to enlist in the U.S. Air Force. It was a big decision to make at that time, to leave my mother and sister alone so soon after my father's death. In retrospect, it was a reasonable decision to make at that time.

For the past decades, I have kept putting one foot forward, held fast to my interests and goals and have invested day after week after year in challenging practices. I have exercised grit. Hopefully, I can continue this practice for the next 9 years or more.

8.   BE TENACIOUS, WORK HARD AND PERSEVERE

As you may know, discipline and persistence are key skills in learning anything, including leadership. Leaders need to constantly practice these skills, just as athletes and musicians practice theirs.

Persistence is probably the single most frequent quality of high achievers. They simply refuse to give up. The longer you hang in there, the greater the chance that something will happen in your favor. No matter how hard it seems, the longer you persist, the more likely you will succeed. This is probably because you are learning from your mistakes and making corrections along the way.

The following are simple rules to follow:

1. Identify the traits and characteristics of discipline and persistence. Then constantly work at developing all aspects of them. Work at it so often that these traits become routine.

2. Take small steps. This will help you to focus on one thing at a time rather than focus on the broader scope. In this way, you will know when you are successful and can move on to the next step.

Terry Fox, having lost his right leg to cancer, embarked on a cross-Canada run called the Marathon of Hope in 1980, to raise money for cancer research. With an artificial leg, his shuffle-and-hop running took him about 26 miles every single day. He covered 3,339 miles from the starting point when he was forced to abandon his Marathon of Hope when doctors discovered cancer in his lungs. He died a few months later, but his inspiring example has left a legacy. He was asked how he kept himself going with thousands of miles ahead of him; he replied, "I just keep running to the next telephone pole."

3. Be consistent because that enables repetition that is at the core of habits. Good habits create a good future.

4. Be persistent in pursuing your goals. Problems, which are always going to pop up, ought not to be reasons to give up. Take the attitude that you will be persistent and will not quit. Celebrate that obstacles are stepping stones to success.

5. Focus on your strength. These are areas of natural talent and require less work to develop. Because of this, it is better to focus on areas where you have natural talent.

6. Stay positive and avoid negative people because, being negative, they will never overcome problems and cannot serve as models for you. What is worse, they may drag you down in their negativity.

7. Seek help and input from your supervisors and fellow employees. The best ideas and support come from these people.

8. Make end results and goals clear—both to others and to yourself. Vague goals and vague end results lead to vague efforts.

9. Gauge how you are progressing with your goals. If you see that success is not likely despite your best efforts and intentions, know when to quit if you assess that things are not working. But you must not come to this conclusion lightly.

Success quotes to be inspired by:

"Most people give up just when they're about to achieve success. They quit on the one-yard line. They give up at the last minute of the game, one foot from a winning touchdown."

— H. Ross Perot, billionaire, former U.S. presidential candidate

"Fall down seven times; get up eight times."

— Japanese proverb

"Persistence and determination alone are omnipotent. The slogan 'press on' has solved and always will solve the problems of the human race."

— Calvin Coolidge, thirtieth president of the United States

"It's always too soon to quit."

— Norman Vincent Peale, inspirational author

"For every failure, there's an alternate course of action. You just have to find it. When you come to a roadblock, take a detour."

— Mary Kay Ash, founder of Mary Kay Cosmetic: "

9. LEARN TO REASON, EXAMINE AND INVESTIGATE ALL THE FACTS

Before you make a decision on any major task, gather all the facts and feedback. This is referred to as due diligence. Observe what is happening around you and train your brain to work to your advantage. To strengthen your observational skills, use the following:

1. Get ready to lay the groundwork and to focus on what matters the most to you. Before you enter a meeting, identify in advance what you want to learn about this group of individuals. Thought helps you to heighten your awareness.

2. Stay in the moment of what is happening now. You should place yourself in the here and now; otherwise, you may miss things in front of you and don't dwell on the past and fret about the future.

3. Flex your mental muscles like you would physically muscles if you were training for a marathon and work toward a goal to be a keen observer.

4. Keep a camera handy to memorialize your everyday environment. If you are speaking to a group, take a few photos to highlight the details around you. By doing so, you will see it again with fresh eyes.

5. If you are doing multi-task jobs, take periodic pauses, you will be less capable of digesting details if you continuously work without a break.

6. Repeat and repeat. You can increase your retention by repeating things over and over. It is recommended to repeat what you want to remember over long intervals to keep it fresh in your mind.

Success quotes to be inspired by:

"Life is like a combination lock; your job is to find the right numbers, in the right order, so you can have anything you want." This is true as long as you can learn to analyze details as described above.

— Brian Tracy, business advisor

"If we did all the things we are capable of doing, we would literally astound ourselves."

— Thomas Edison, inventor

"People who are wrapped up in themselves make small packages."

— Benjamin Franklin, statesman, inventor, businessman

"No matter how things are for you, they're harder for other people, and if you stick to it, you can get around the brick walls in your life."

— Sonia Sotomayor, Associate Justice of the US Supreme Court

10. FOCUS ON YOUR FUTURE

A simple concept has it that you ought to "say *no* to the good so that you can say *yes* to the great."

Even the top entrepreneurs, professionals, educators and civic leaders get caught up in projects and situations that are merely good, while the great is left out-in-the-cold. This prevents the great from showing up in your life because you've spent all of your time accomplishing the good. This dynamic occurs far too often.

If you survey your life and record those activities that brought you success, financial gains, the most advancement, the most joy, you would discover about 20% of your activities produces about 80% of your success. This is called the "Pareto Principle," named after the famous Italian economist, Vilfredo Pareto.

Instead of watching television, surfing the internet, running unnecessary errands, just goofing off, you could use the extra time to focus on your family, marriage, business, courses, a new income stream and other productive pursuits.

To determine what is truly great from what is good, make use of the following ideas:

1. **Start by listing your opportunities**. Use the left side of the page to list the good and the right side for the great. Writing these opportunities down on paper will aid your overall thinking ability about the subject.

2. **Talk to a mentor about your idea**. People and mentors may have traveled this road before and have vast experience to share and hard questions to ask. They can offer you valuable insights to help you determine if you are on the right road.

3. **Test the water**. Conduct a small test, spend limited time and money. If it is a new career, first seek part time work. If you plan to move to a new city, first see if you can travel for a few months to your dream location. Also, before buying a home, rent for a few months to see if you like the neighborhood, the house and the neighbors.

4. **Focus on where you spend your time**. See if these activities truly serve your goals. If they do not, you have extra free time to schedule great pursuits.

11. NOW, IT IS TIME TO FOCUS ON MONEY INSTEAD OF TIME.

With reference to money, financial success starts in the mind. You have to decide what you want, that you deserve it, visualize it and be willing to pay the price to get it. With disciplined effort, perseverance and hard work over time, you can achieve your financial goals.

Most people never get to the first stages of accumulating wealth. They are limited by their own belief about money. The basic reason is that people are not taught about wealth-creation or money management in school, instead they focus on careers, assuming that money will follow later.

It takes time to become wealthy; you must invest effort and hard work. Also, you will need to identify, root out and replace any negative beliefs about money that you learned during childhood. The saying such as "the little guy can't get ahead," "Money doesn't grow on trees," "There's not enough money to go around," "You have to have money to make money" may influence your thinking as you mature. These thoughts are not true. If you believe them, they will eventually prevent you from being financially successful.

You can change your early programmed thoughts about money by using the following three steps to turn around your limiting belief about money:

1. Write down your limiting beliefs: "Money is the root of all evil," "Better to be happy than rich," etc.

2. Challenge and argue with the limiting belief by brainstorming a list of new beliefs that counter the old limiting ones. Write them in the positive.

3. Create a turnaround statement that is opposite from the original beliefs. Repeat them often.

Do you know how much wealth you want? If you haven't determined your vision, be sure you prepare a written goal or goals such as the following:

- I will have a new worth of $_____ by MONTH and YEAR.
- I will earn $_____ by next year at this time.
- I will save and invest $_____ every month.
- I will start the new financial habit of _____.

Get serious about your retirement as early in life as possible. You need to know how much money you will need to maintain your current lifestyle after you stop working. Charles Schwab suggests that for every $1,000 in monthly income, you will need about $230,000 invested when you retire. This is referred to as your "nest-egg." Whether that is enough, will depend on your projected retirement cashflow needs, your projected additional income sources; Social Security, other pensions, rental income, etc.

Remember: "If your outflow exceeds your income... Your upkeep will be your downfall."

To become conscious about your money and to be financially successful, you need to know where you want to go and how to get there. The following step will help to achieve this journey.

1. **Determine your net worth**. This includes everything that is liquid or could be turned into liquid assets. Bank accounts, mutual funds, real estate, possessions.

2. **Determine what you need to retire**. This can include "must have" and "nice to have." Make sure the "nice to have" is based on your interests and living habits. There is no need to stress yourself with not having what

society thinks you should have. Being financially independent will free you up to pursue your passion, travel or whatever it is you want to do.

3. **Become aware of what you spend**. Most people don't know how much they spend each month. Keep a monthly record of expenditures. Obviously, you cannot spend more than you earn. Do not make up the difference with credit card debt. It is a losing habit.

4. **Enhance the prospect of becoming financially literate** by taking courses. Professor Robert Kawasaki said, "We were not taught financial literacy in school. It takes a lot of work and time to change your thinking and to become financial literate."

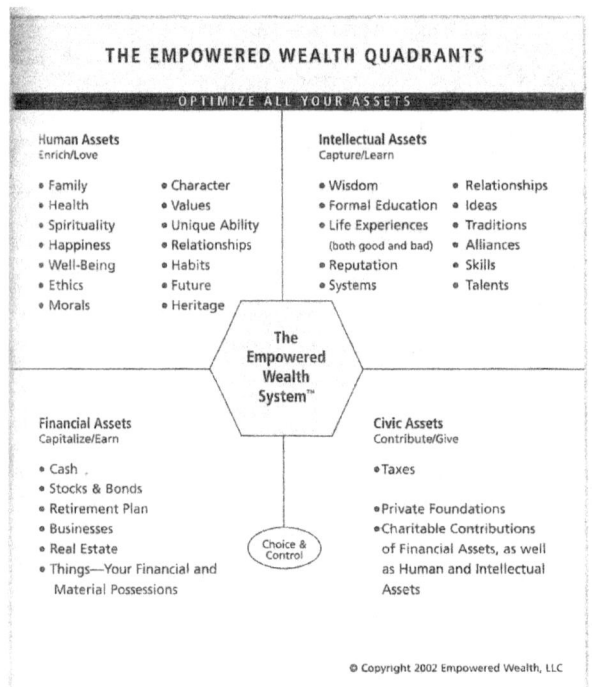

© Copyright 2002 Empowered Wealth, LLC

It would behoove wealthy families to look closely at each asset to maximize and pass on the assets in all four quadrants to the next and subsequent generations. By doing so, you will keep money in its proper perspective.

Please study the following "The Empowered Wealth Quadrant" chart, on this page.

Success quotes to be inspired by:

"The man without a purpose is like a ship without a rudder—a waif, a nothing, a no man."

— Thomas Carlyle, English writer

"The number one problem in today's generation and economy is the lack of financial literacy."

— Alex Greenspan, former chairman of the Federal Reserve Board

12. DON'T BE AFRAID TO BE DIFFERENT, MAKE CHANGES AND TO HAVE QUALITIES CONSIDERED IMPROPER BY THE MANY.

Following the herd is a sure path to mediocrity. Instead of seeking out those who can show you how to repeat what is currently making the rounds, seek out those who you feel have better answers—not popular answers.

To cut through the noise, you have to become a good listener of what your instinct tells you is the better way. If you are not a great listener become one because you can gather more facts and inspirations while with others by listening to them rather than spouting your opinions which teaches you nothing. Those people who continuously talk do not learn. Admittedly, it is not easy to keep quiet and listen, but it is to your advantage to do so. By listening and capturing more of what people say that is unique and important, you increase the rate of your learning process.

To become an effective listener, use the following procedures:

1. **Embrace Mindfulness**. Most people would listen better if they had quieter minds, minds that weren't always busy formulating opinions and rebuttals. How to do this?

Embracing mindfulness is actually not so hard. On a regular daily basis—and certainly before an important meeting, take five minutes to sit quietly and ignore distractions. Many mindfulness practitioners count their breaths—in and out: one; in and out: two. You will be surprised at how even so short a mindful period can quiet your mind which will help you to focus better. Once you have mastered the habit of taking five minutes, try longer periods. How does that work for you?

2. **Set the stage.** If you want to pick someone's brain, it is very useful to make a list of questions you would like to have answers to by the time you are through with your meeting. Right before the meeting, do a five-minute mindfulness session. In the meeting, if you have an option, choose a position to sit or stand that is near the speaker and makes possible direct eye contact. Keep your introductory remarks brief. You are not there to tell the other person how wonderful and important you are.

Once the person begins to speak—that is, to talk about the subject you have come to learn more about, concentrate on what is being said. This will make it easier to digest every word the other person says. Give appropriate feedback. Nod your head yes. Smile appreciatively. Say short sentences like: "That's amazing! "Oh, I see." Every once in a while, you can ask a question to make sure you understand what is being said. Determine if taking notes is in order, and if it is, you ought to take as many as you need to recall the conversation in detail.

Do not cut-in or interrupt. In fact, nothing says excellent listener more than the absence of interrupting the speaker. Instead of cutting in, good listeners prefer to keep their mouths closed and their ears open.

At the end of the session, if it is appropriate, you can scan your questions to see if any remain unanswered. It is also possible to mirror back to the speaker what you have learned in the time you were together. This gives the speaker the opportunity to add to or correct what you have given as feedback. Clearly this is to your advantage if you have come as a student.

Listen with the goal to empathize with the speaker. If your goal is to form an alliance with the speaker rather than to pick his or her brain, the listening skills expressed in #2 are all great, but there is something to add.

That needed addition is empathy. Make such comments as "Oh, that must have been difficult!" or "You were wonderful. I admire your effort!" Repeat the speaker's words. This is called mirroring and is effective in creating rapport. "So, you found the solution for retrieving all you had lost."

Non-verbal communication counts for much. To the ones that have already been mentioned above, you can add smiling, pursing your lips, making gestures. All of these tell the speaker, "I'm with you."

Body language also counts for much. Speakers tend to open up to listeners using body language that mirrors theirs. If appropriate, also mirror the speaker's body language and gestures. If she sits crossed legged, sit cross legged yourself. If he leans forward, lean forward. This will help the speaker to feel affiliated with you. (However, be careful not to be too obvious, or else you may pass as mimicking the person.)

13. IN A COMPANY SETTING, LET OTHERS DO THE SPEAKING.

If at a company meeting, rather than presenting new ideas in an elaborate slide show, share your ideas with the gathering in a five-minute stand-up talk. This will allow employees to speak about their approach and can very well come up with alternate solutions.

So, listen up and don't blabber.

Success quotes to be inspired by:

"Invention requires a long-term willingness to be misunderstood."

— Jeff Bezos, Amazon founder and CEO

"Nothing else can quite substitute for a few well-chosen, well timed, sincere words of praise."

— Sam Walton, Wal-Mart founder

14. BARGAIN EFFECTIVELY WITH PEOPLE

Mastering the art of persuasion will provide you with a competitive edge as you bargain with people. Even in this age of computer technology and artificial intelligence, effective communication skills are essential and are the number one skill that is lacking in our daily lives.

To become a better communicator, make use of the following tips to persuade people in the bargaining process:

1. Keep your presentation's vocabulary basic. Great persuaders use simple words to explain complex ideas. Unless you know your audience well, you must suppose that many people you are speaking to do not understand your subject as well as you do. When you add to this challenge of concept the complexity of vocabulary, you have the makings of confusion. Confusion may well lead to your audience dropping out.

2. Use stories to get your idea(s) across. Stories are the simple best tool to render an idea intelligible to another person. To paraphrase the old adage of "a picture is worth a thousand words," we could say "a tight, pertinent story is worth a thousand essay words." Craft your story so that there is a problem expressed and then there is a solution that you can bring to bear with a service or product.

3. Pace your presentation. Studies have shown that, generally, people tune out at a lecture after about 10 minutes. While this will certainly be different for different audiences, it is safe to safe that you would do well to re-engage your audience with a new story. This story might highlight how a client or customer was struggling unsuccessfully with a problem or part of a problem and how a specific solution was brought to bear to change the problem into a successful resolution.

4. Be genuine. When you speak from your experience and knowledge, you will come across as honest. Honesty is the best policy. If you are not honest, sooner or later the truth will come out. Honesty leads the audience to view you as genuine—the real thing. Being genuine is the best policy because people will sense that they know where they stand with you. This will leave them free to evaluate the content of your presentation rather than you.

5. Acknowledge people. We all love to be recognize for our achievements or at least for our efforts if achievements did not follow. Offer people a pat on the back for a job well done. It's even better if you can do this in public so that others can participate in acknowledging the individual.

6. Be Polite. In conversations and in e-mails, always express yourself in polite terms. Show respect.

Success quotes to be inspired by:

"I've worked hard and too long to let anything stand in the way of my goals. I will not let my teammates down and I will not let myself down."

— Mia Hamm, Olympic athlete

"There are no secrets to success. It is the result of preparation, hard work and learning from failure."

— Colin Powell, U.S. Army general and Secretary of State

"Of all the properties which belong to honorable men, not one is so highly prized as that of character."

— Henry Clay, American statesman

"Judge a man by his questions rather than his answers."

— Voltaire, French philosopher

"Never doubt that a small group of thoughtful, committed citizens can change the world. Indeed, it is the only thing that ever has."

— Margaret Mead, American cultural anthropologist

"Genuine politics … is simply a matter of serving those around us: serving the community and serving those who will come after us. Its deepest roots are moral because it is a responsibility expressed through action, to and for the whole."

— Vaclav Havel, Czech statesman, last president of Czechoslovakia:

"Anything done for another is done for oneself."

— Pope John Paul II

"For those to whom much is given, much is required. And when, at some future date, the high court of history sits in judgment on each of us, recording whether in our brief span of service we fulfilled our responsibilities to the state, our success or failure, in whatever office we hold, will be measured by the answers to four questions:

- First, were we truly men of courage?
- Second, were we truly men of judgment?
- Third, were we truly men of integrity?
- Finally, were we truly men of dedication?"

— John F. Kennedy, 35th US President

"Unless someone like you cares a whole awful lot, nothing is going to get better. It's not."

— Dr. Seuss, writer

"They say that time changes things, but you actually have to change them yourself."

— Andy Warhol, artist

15. BE A STRAIGHT SHOOTER

Here are suggestions to become a straight shooter:

1. **Be truly helpful**. If a friend asks for help and you accept the invitation, it is important to tell the truth to that person whether it's something the person wants to hear or not.

2. **Develop moral strength**. Develop character to handle the truth about yourself when it comes your way. If you don't have character to face the truth, the other stuff that you discuss doesn't matter. Your decision will be based on shaky ground; you will not be able to execute effectively.

3. **Be open to all possibilities when talking with people**. Discuss the problem in a way that shows that you are earnest, humble, positive and genuine. This may include hearing negative comments about you or about your approach to the problem.

Success quotes to be inspired by:

"Success is measured not so much by the position that one has reached in life as by the obstacles which he has overcome."

— Booker T. Washington, educator

"Our greatest weakness lies in giving up. The most certain way to succeed is always to try just one more time."

— Thomas Edison, inventor

"Do not let what you cannot do interfere with what you can do."

— John Wooden, basketball coach, UCLA, 10 NCAA championships

"The search for a scapegoat is the easiest of all hunting expeditions."

— Dwight Eisenhower, 34th president of the US

"Truth is like a lion. You don't have to defend it. Let it loose, and it will defend itself."

— St. Augustine, Biblical scholar quoting Second Timothy 1:14

725 Starbush Dr.

Sunnyvale, California 94086

July 17, 2012

Dear Pauline,

I would like to take this opportunity to thank you for the part you played in helping me to achieve my current status in life.

Although many people have influenced my life, you were one of the first. As an older sister, to myself and Christine, you filled in when our parents were working out in the fields. You were instrumental in providing a wholesome, stable and inspirational upbringing and a pleasant lifestyle.

You reinforced our parent's teachings on Integrity, personal discipline, social skills, courage, hard work, perseverance and focus.

Again, thank you for caring for me during my early life while our mother was working in the fields, encouraging me to excel in school, being available for advice and counsel, being my mentor even though you didn't know I was watching you're ever move, encouraging me during difficult times while in the military and later in civilian life and continuing to be an inspiration to me during our weekly Saturday conversations. These features culminated into a better and fulfilling life for me knowing that I have done my best and not straying from the above basic principles learned early in life.

Wishing you a long and healthy life! I love you for being the person that you are.

Your youngest brother,

Love,

Everett

725 Starbush Dr.

Sunnyvale, California 94086

October 15, 2015

Dear Pauline,

It is fitting and proper that I recognize and celebrate you for living to be 95 years and six months as of this date. Congratulation! I have fond memories of you when you cared for me as an infant, nurtured me until I finished high school, mentored me as an adult while in the Air Force and in my civilian career plus being an inspiration to me during our weekly phone conversations, for the past 20 to 25 years.

I well remember our humble beginning where we raised our food and livestock on the farm for existence. We were a close net family who cared and helped each member as need arise. Who would have guessed that this little "awkward boy" from the sticks of Kentucky would grow up to graduate in the top of his high school class, be in the top 1% of his peers of the Air Force, have a successful career in the Aerospace Industry, and an active real estate business? I give you credit for encouraging me to succeed in life and to use my talent to go as far as possible. You stressed that success is accomplished through hard work, determination and perseverance. I thank you for all you have done for me during my lifetime and I will always be grateful. You will always be in my thoughts and prayers wherever our paths lead us.

I wish you many more years of peace, happiness and contentment the rest of your life. May God bless you!

Love,

Everett,

Your Youngest Brother

(Note: My sister died two or three weeks after I wrote this letter.)

725 Starbush Drive

Sunnyvale, California 94086

April 20, 2020

Dear Christine,

I guess that you are surprised to be getting a letter from me since I usually call you each Sunday afternoon to catch-up and to check on your health and well-being.

Routine calls are good but it becomes necessary to write occasionally to re-enforce our close relationship as a brother and sister. Do you remember when we were young when I built a sled for us to ride down the snow cap hill behind our home? On one of the rides, you almost broke your finger but eventually it was only a bruise and a skinned finger. Also, do you remember when you broke your arm when you fell out of the cherry tree in front of the house? You were wearing a sling for months. Since we made most of our toys, we were able to entertain ourselves by keeping busy, playing leap frog and anti-over. The anti-over was an interesting sport when we would throw a ball over the house, the person on the other side would catch the ball and run around fast enough to hit the other person with the ball. We mostly played with our close relatives, Bonny, Denver, Herbert and whoever was available at the time, when we were not working in our daily chores.

I want to thank you and Frank for visiting me during my college graduation in Hawaii. This was a most memorable occasion for the entire family. Mary Ann was reasonably well at the time and we were able to visit some of the historic sites on the island. Additionally, I am grateful for your effort in caring for our mother when she had a stroke and during her long stay in the retirement home.

Soon, you will be embarking on a significant change in your lifestyle by moving from your home, of many years, to a permanent long-time care facility. This is a bold endeavor in which you may experience many ups-and-downs. From a long perspective and with your declining health, this seems to be best course of action at this time. I wish you well and many more healthy years.

Remember, we are the only two remaining members of the original Woolum Family of 13 siblings. We've had a great life. Let's keep this legacy going for many more years?

Your youngest brother!

Love always,

Everett

725 Starbush Drive

Sunnyvale, California 94086

October 4, 2002

I did not have the opportunity to speak with Virgil, before his death. If I had, I would have thanked him for the many things he taught me, the fun we had growing up together, and for all the things he helped me throughout my life. I would have also told him that I admired him and his decision-making, and that he was a role-model as I planned out my life. We were very close. I wrote a brief note (see below) and included it in the casket after his funeral.

Final Good-bye Note

I would like to say a final good-by to you (Virgil) and to thank you for all the encouragement you have given me through the years. You have been my mentor and have emphasized through the years the following traits: Integrity, Personal Discipline, Social Skills, Grit, Perseverance, and Goal-setting. If you recall that our father taught us to be honest, dependable and trustworthy. He would always say, "My Word is My Bond."

The previous traits were great but the close friendship I had with you will never be forgotten. I could discuss any subject, at any time of the day, without any hesitation. Even though you were several years older, at times I would consider you like a father and other times a dear close brother. I will surely miss you.

Rest in peace and I will see you on the other side.

Your youngest brother,

Everett

725 Starbush Drive

Sunnyvale, California 94086

April 15, 2020

Dear Rosita,

I want to send you a belated Easter Greeting. Because of the COVID-19 restrictions, most people in California and other parts of the country have been restricted to staying at home. I have been accustomed to talking with you on a weekly basis but since Vivanne cannot visit to originate the call, I have to resort to writing.

It has been almost three weeks since I have spoken with you. I hope that you are doing very well and have not had any symptoms of the coronavirus. California has been hit very hard, thousands hospitalized and many deaths. So far, the officials do not know the final outcome and are very cautious. Our economy has come to a crawl, only the necessary activities are functioning.

On a positive note, I would like to remind you of the many wonderful trips we made together overseas and throughout America. Do you remember when we took your mother to Mexico? Her only means of getting around was in a wheelchair but she was determined to go to the restaurant we always went to in Tijuana. It was a difficult time pushing her through the rough streets in that city. As I recall, your mother was living with your brother at the time, and he did not know that we had taken her. The trip was successful, and we got her back home safely. I could remind you of many trips we took together which were educational and inspirational. We were always looking for new adventures.

I miss you very much. Before you left for Seattle in November 2015, you would always call me each evening to see if I had arrived home safely and call me the first thing in the morning, to plan the activities for the day.

During the years of our friendship, you were an inspiration to me. You expanded my thinking and "brought me out of my shell." You shared your experiences relating to world cultures, art, music, and finances, with me. As you shared your worldviews and. you expanded mine, I became a better person. We talked freely and had similar goals in life. Even though we worked hard in our real estate business, we made time to enjoy life, travel, raise dogs, birds, rabbits, tended to the orchard and many other activities.

Be safe! I hope to talk with you soon.

Your friend!

Love,

Everett.

Summary

When I wrote the previous pages, I lived alone, in the house my wife and I purchased in 1975. I earned my living by serving 26 years in the military and working 26 years in the Aerospace Industry. I have lived in my current home for over 40 years. I have had many wonderful memories here. Also, some life-altering ones, as my children left home, and when my wife, Mary Ann, died in 1988.

I would like to thank the military and the aerospace industry, my family, friends and distant relatives for providing me with the guidance, wisdom and life experiences that led me to have the life I've enjoyed. They all played a significant role in the successes in my life.

This Memoir, in a sense, is my final major assessment as I look back at my life. Most of my years are in the rear-view-mirror and now I have but a short time before I reach the end of my travels. I came across an essay that has caused me to stop, think, and evaluate the things I've done. I'd like to share it with you:

What Will Matter

By

Michael Josephson

Ready or not, some day it will all come to an end.

There will be no more sunrises, no minutes, hours or days.

All the things you collected, whether treasured or forgotten, will pass to someone else. Your wealth, fame and temporal power will shrivel to irrelevance.

It will not matter what you owned or what you were owed.

Your grudges, resentments, frustrations and jealousies will finally disappear.

So too, your hopes, ambitions, plans and to-do lists will expire.

The wins and losses that once seemed so important will fade away.

It won't matter where you came from, or what side of the tracks you lived on at the end.

It won't matter whether you were beautiful or brilliant.

Even your gender and skin color will be irrelevant.

So, what will matter? How will the value of your days be measured?

What will matter is not what you bought but what you built,

not what you got but what you gave.

What will matter is not your success but your significance.

What will matter is not what you learned but what you taught.

What will matter is every act of integrity, compassion, courage or sacrifice that

enriched, empowered or encouraged others to emulate your example.

What will matter is not your competence, but your character.

What will matter is not how many people you knew,

but how many will feel a lasting loss when you're gone.

What will matter is not your memories but the memories of those who loved you.

What will matter is how long you will be remembered, by whom and for what.

Living a life that matters doesn't happen by accident.

It's not a matter of circumstance but of choice.

Choose to live a life that matters.

I think that this essay accurately represents my world-view. It summarizes my thoughts about the things that really matter in life. I hope that you will reflect on the words, and allow the message to sink-in.

At the present, I continue working with real-estate for the benefit of myself, my family, and others. Nearing the end of this long journey, I have re-visited my childhood experiences, described my military and in aerospace careers, discussed my challenges, reflected on leadership and moral principles, outlined my thoughts on success, and recounted some of my travel experiences. All of these things have become an integral part of who I am.

The main purpose of this memoir is to leave a record of my story, to explain the periods and events that shaped my life, to expound on the many things that motivated and molded me. To leave a record that you can use as a guide in building your own legacy. I have attempted to describe each activity truthfully, with as much detail as I remember, in order to help you in that endeavor.

Anais Nin writes: *"We write to heighten our own awareness of life. We write to taste life twice, in the moment and in retrospection. We write to be able to transcend our life, to reach beyond it, to teach ourselves to speak with others, to record the journey into the labyrinth."*

The major theme of my memoir is my discussion of success. It is to work hard, to have passion for your job, to have an open-mind, to be challenged by others who have a better understanding of a subject, to listen to the wisdom of people God has placed in your life. I've tried to summarize my observations in the 15 principles of success. I believe that as you follow the principles I've outlined, and after much prayer, God gives you "a peaceful feeling" about your petition, then, you can confidently follow through with your plan.

I believe that the confidence instilled in a person, after quiet and reflective prayer in consultation with the Lord is what leads to that unwavering focus that I call Grit. It is what allows us to persevere through the difficult, sometime painful phases of life. Grit allows us to "finish the good race, striving for the finish-line, onward to our goal" in the hope of hearing, once we finish.... "Well done, good and faithful servant!"

We are "At the End of the Day", the person that we chose to become. The choice is to follow God's leading or to follow "the world's". Your choices and inclinations will determine your final result. As for me, I will continue to obey the covenant I have with God, to follow His guidance and his commands, the rest of my days. I know that there are brighter days ahead for each of us.

"You see in the final analysis; it is between you and God. It was never between you and them anyway."

Mother Teresa

Thank you, may God always bless you.

Everett Woolum

HISTORY OF MY DNA

DNA is described as any of the class of nucleic acids that functions in the transference of genetic characteristics. It is also called deoxyribonucleic acid, the molecule that contains the genetic code of organisms.

My DNA tells the story of who I am and how I am connected to the population around the world. It traces my heritage throughout the centuries and uncovers clues about where and when my ancestors lived.

The following is a summary of my origin and migration:

European – 99.1% (65.3% British & Irish, United Kingdom, Ireland), (16.1% French & German), (1.7% Scandinavian, (1.6% Spanish & Portuguese), (13.4% Broadly Northwestern European), (0.9% Broadly Southern European), (0.1% Broadly European).

Sub-Saharan Africa – (0.8% Ghanaian, Liberian & Sierra Leonean).

East Asian & Native American – (0.1% Broadly Northern Asian & Native American.

GALLERY OF EXTRA PHOTOS

2006, Everett with Yugoslavian girls

2006, Switzerland

2006, Yugoslavia, Rosita on Tito's train

2007, Trip to Top of Europe

2011, Netherlands

2013, Ushuaia, Argentina

2018- Everett on another adventure, flying over the San Francisco Bay Area

2018, Everett at Mary Ann's grave

2018, Jesus Burial tomb

Adventure on Yantze River - China 2012

Black Sea, 2006

Brazil 2013

Christ the Redeemer, Brazil. 2013

Copa Cabana, Brazil 2013

China 2012

Greece, 2018

Heading-out, 2015

Norway, 2015

Cusco, Peru.   2013

Dead Sea - Israel 2018

Everett at his home

Everett at Parent's gravesite

Everett in Santorini, 2018

Everett retirement ceremony

Everett with friend, Olivia. Chile, 2013

Everett, desk where he wrote his memoir

Iguazu Falls, Argentina side, 2013

Jesus Placed His Hand There -2000 Years Ago

Kaitlin Woolum, grand-niece, 2020

Luxembourg American Military Cemetery, 2007

Machu Picchu walls 2013

Machu Picchu, Peru 2013

Maudie, Christine. Circa 1960

Mt of Olives, Israel. 2018

Netherlands, 2007

Nova Scotia - Canada, 2019

Original Olympic stadium, Greece

Picking Chinese Tea Leaves 2012

Romania 2006

Rosita on Black Sea trip

Rosita, Gus, Everett. 2019

Samuel Woolum, headstone

Sarah Woolum, grand-niece, 2020

SSgt Woolum

Stake where Apostle Paul was flogged

Terra-cotta Soldiers 2012

Tiananmen Square 2012

Trans-Atlantic cruise 2019, friends Richard and Carolyn Hay

Travis AFB, CA

Virgil Pauline Christine Everett

Virgil, Christine, Pauline, Everett, Circa 1993

Wailing Wall - Israel 2018

Everett Woolum

www.ingramcontent.com/pod-product-compliance
Lightning Source LLC
Chambersburg PA
CBHW071752120626
46550CB00002B/758